In Canadian Service Aircraft

Boeing CC137
(707-347C)

Photo Opposite: CC137 tanker refuelling two CF-5A aircraft while a third stands by.
(Richard J. De Launais)

In Canadian Service Aircraft

Boeing CC137
(707-347C)

Anthony L. Stachiw
Andrew Tattersall

Vanwell Publishing Limited
St. Catharines, Ontario

Copyright © 2004   Anthony L. Stachiw and Andrew Tattersall

All rights reserved. No part of this book may be reproduced or used in any form or by any means, electronic or mechanical, including photocopying, recording, or in any information storage and retrieval system, without permission in writing from the publisher.

Vanwell Publishing acknowledges the financial support of the Government of Canada through the Book Publishing Industry Development Program for our publishing activities.

Vanwell Publishing Limited
1 Northrup Crescent
P.O. Box 2131
St. Catharines, Ontario L2R 7S2
sales@vanwell.com
tel: 905-937-3100
fax: 905-937-1760
Printed in Canada

Cover and Book Design by Renée Giguère
Cover Illustration by Stephen Otvos

Library and Archives Canada Cataloguing in Publication

Stachiw, A. L. (Anthony L.), 1940-
    Boeing CC137 : (707-347C) / Anthony L. Stachiw, Andrew Tattersall.

(In Canadian service. Aircraft ; 2)
Includes bibliographical references.
ISBN 1-55125-079-9

    1. Boeing 707 (Jet transports) 2. Canada. Canadian Armed Forces–Aviation. 3. Jet transports–Canada. I. Tattersall, Andrew, 1971- II. Title. III. Series.

TL686.B65S73 2004   358.4'4'0971   C2004-903172-4

CONTENTS

CHAPTER ONE
Origins of the Design: Boeing Model 367-80 7

CHAPTER TWO
The CC137 in Canadian Service 16

CHAPTER THREE
Aircraft Description and Drawings 25

CHAPTER FOUR
CC137 Squadrons and Units 54

CHAPTER FIVE
CC137 Colour Schemes and Markings 58

CHAPTER SIX
Air-to-Air Refuelling System 71

CHAPTER SEVEN
Canadian Forces and the NATO AWACS 80

CHAPTER EIGHT
Long Range Patrol Aircraft 85

CHAPTER NINE
Modelling the Boeing CC137 and NATO E-3 Sentry AWACS 91

ACKNOWLEDGEMENTS

There are several people whose assistance has been instrumental in the writing of this book. I would, once again, like to thank John Griffin, the noted authority on Canadian military aircraft and author of several books on the subject, for his encouragement and support. As well, John Turanchik, with his keen eye for detail has, over the years, provided clippings from newspapers and magazines whenever he spotted material relevant to the CC137 aircraft. Harry Turpin provided data on the CC137 fleet disposal as well as the aircraft configuration as they were offered for sale, and A.J. Barnhardt provided CC137 publications that were used as reference for details on the aircraft and its systems.

The staff of The Canadian Forces Joint Imagery Centre, A Squadron, Department of National Defence, in particular Janet Lacroix and WO Steve Sauvé, provided assistance and direction in the procurement of the photographs. The approval for their use was expedited by Armanda Tomei of the Department of National Defence, Directorate of Intellectual Property. Andrew Cline, Richard De Launais, Patrick Martin and Bill Scobie have provided photographs from their extensive collections. Patrick Martin's publication on Canadian Armed Forces, Aircraft Finish & Markings, 1968-1997, was used as an indispensable guide in writing Chapter 5, CC137 Colour Schemes and Markings.

For Chapter 9 on Modelling the Boeing CC137, Bill Scobie provided photographs of his excellent model, and Dave Koss of Leading Edge Models and James Botaitis of JBOT Decals provided information on their decal products depicting the markings for the CC137.

Finally, thanks to Simon Kooter of Vanwell Publishing for providing the opportunity to present this book, and to Angela Dobler, the editor, for her expertise in its preparation.

CHAPTER ONE

Origins of the Design Boeing Model 367-80

The Boeing Model 367-80 on the ramp at the Boeing facility in Renton, Washington undergoing pre-flight inspection during early flight testing.
(Museum of Flight Collection, Seattle Washington)

Boeing CC137 (707-347C)

Following the Second World War, the airlines became increasingly popular with the traveling public who were attracted by the safety and efficiency of this relatively new mode of transportation. The aircraft then in use were, for the most part, piston engine powered conversions of ex-military transports. The majority of these were Douglas DC-3Cs, which were converted ex-military C-47s. Alternately, the airlines flew developments of those military designs, such as the Douglas DC-4, a civilian version of the C-54 Skymaster. Improvements were gradually made to the airliners, such as pressurization of the passenger cabin, allowing flight at higher altitudes and bringing about modest improvement in travel comfort. However, that comfort was often limited by the high noise levels and the inability of the aircraft to fly high enough to escape the effects of the weather. The limit of development of the piston engine powered airliners came with the introduction of the second generation, such as the Boeing Stratocruiser, Lockheed L1049G Super Constellation, or the Douglas DC-7. These were in turn eclipsed by the ultimate in propeller driven airliners, the Bristol Britannia turboprop airliner, allowing travel at much higher altitude and greater speeds.

With the introduction of the jet engine in the Second World War, great advances were realized in aircraft performance, enabling flight at speeds and altitudes previously unimagined. These advances, initially, were restricted to military aircraft, since the early turbine engines had neither the reliability nor efficiency to warrant their application to civil air transports. The British had embarked upon a program to develop a jet powered transport aircraft in the late 1940s which resulted in the graceful DeHavilland DH-106 Comet 1, which went into commercial service in 1952. However, two fatal accidents occurred, caused by metal fatigue, as investigation determined. This resulted in explosive decompression of the aircraft cabin and disintegration of the aircraft at high altitude. Pending corrective modifications to the aircraft, the Comet fleet was temporarily withdrawn from service. The Comet was later reintroduced into service, and an advanced variant, the Comet 4 was introduced into trans-Atlantic service in 1958.

In Canada, the Avro Aircraft Company of Canada Ltd. had designed and produced the prototype of their C-102 Jetliner. The aircraft offered excellent performance, in spite of being denied state of the art jet engines. Nevertheless, it attracted orders from a major American airline. It finally faded into obscurity when priority was placed on the manufacture of the CF100 Canuck all-weather interceptor fighters for Canada's air defence. In retrospect, it can probably be safely concluded that lack of government support, compounded by subtle intervention by the British and American aviation industry to scuttle this threat to their dominance of the world market in airliners, had an affect on the decision.

In the United States, the Boeing Aircraft Company had begun production of the B-47 Stratojet and the B-52 Stratofortress jet powered strategic bombers. This experience was put to good use when the company initiated design studies for a jet powered airliner. On 30 August 1952 Boeing announced that it was investing $16 million of company money to build the prototype of a new jet powered transport aircraft. Early concepts bore a superficial resemblance to the Boeing Stratocruiser piston engine powered airliner that Boeing had produced post-war, and which was a development of the B-29 Superfortress Second World War bomber. Four jet engines were mounted in pairs in pods slung forward of and underneath the wings on pylons, as on the B-47 and B-52. The wings could be kept aerodynamically clean and the engines would be removed as far as possible from the fuel tanks in the wings. A change was made to mount each engine singly, since, in the paired arrangement, both engines could be damaged in the event of the explosion of either engine. As well, the pod arrangement facilitated maintaining and servicing the engines. The pods were spaced evenly along the span of the wing to distribute the weight evenly.

The early wing design, of moderate sweep back, was replaced by a high aspect ratio flexible swept back wing which was based on B-47 and B-52 experience. This wing shape not only possessed good high speed characteristics, but incorporated advanced high lift devices and controls to improve takeoff performance and low speed control. In light of the sad experience of the DeHavilland Comet, and the resulting skepticism of the airlines in the safety of high speed, high altitude jet powered airliners, the fuselage was designed to incorporate high resistance to structural failure. Exhaustive testing was done in facilities specially designed for that purpose. A unique four wheel main landing gear and a dual wheel nose landing gear were designed to accommodate the stresses of high speed takeoff and landing. The main gear trucks retracted inwards into the wing centre section, and the nose gear retracted forward into the underside of the aircraft nose.

CHAPTER ONE

The prototype Model 367-80 N70700 at Boeing Field, 13 July 1990, after its return from storage for refurbishment. *(Patrick Martin)*

The thousands of hours of design studies and testing resulted in the prototype Boeing Model 367-80, registration N70700. The aircraft was unveiled in a ceremony at the company plant at Renton, Washington on 15 May 1954. The first flight was on 15 July 1954, piloted by A.M. "Tex" Johnston, and copilot R.X. "Dix" Loesch. In the words of the pilot, the initial one hour and twenty-four minute flight "went without a hitch". Flight testing continued on the Stratoliner, as every aspect of her flight characteristics were investigated. Over the years, the 367-80 was modified many times, undergoing structural and aerodynamic changes in the course of developing and testing advanced features of other models of Boeing aircraft. Included were new wing planforms and airfoils, powerplant modifications, entirely new wing leading and trailing edge flaps, and, for the 727 model, an aft mounted engine test pod. The aircraft continued in use as a flying test laboratory until its last flight in May 1972 when it was turned over to the Smithsonian Institution in Washington, D.C. It was subsequently returned from storage in the Arizona desert to Boeing in May 1990 where volunteer labour restored the aircraft to new condition. The refurbished 367-80 made a special fly-over of Boeing facilities in July 1991 to commemorate the seventy-fifth anniversary of the Boeing Company and the thirty-seventh anniversary of its own first flight, and is now on view at Boeing Field.

BOEING 707 MILITARY VARIANTS

Although the military had initially shown little interest in the aircraft, after experiencing convincing demonstration flights, they reacted enthusiastically to its spectacular performance. In July 1954, the USAF ordered into production a version designated Model 717 which went into service as the KC-135 Stratotanker, an aerial refueling tanker for the Strategic Air Command bomber fleet. This was to replace the propeller driven Boeing KC-97, which was itself a military development of the Boeing Stratocruiser. This original version was powered by the JT-3C (military J-57) turbojet engines and designated KC-135A. The first aircraft entered service in 1957 with the last being delivered in 1965. In all some 732 tankers were built, and by 2003, some 550 still remain in service.

Boeing CC137 (707-347C)

The KC-135 was equipped with a streamlined "flying boom" aerial refuelling system that had been perfected on the 367-80 prototype. Fuel tanks were located in the lower level of the two deck fuselage, and in the wings, allowing the use of the upper deck for personnel or cargo transport. Access to the unobstructed upper deck was through a single large cargo door in the forward port side of the fuselage.

A major program to replace lower wing surfaces and engine strut fittings on 746 C/KC-135 aircraft was completed in 1988. The majority of the aircraft modified in the thirteen-year program were tankers. The replacement skinning involved the use of an aluminum alloy that was less susceptible to fatigue.

Starting in 1981, the USAF began an engine retrofit program for the KC-135A fleet. Retired civilian 707B models were purchased for cannibalization, their JT-3D/TF33-102 turbofan engines being used to replace the existing JT-3C/J-57 engines. After being modified, the aircraft, totalling 161 airframes, were designated KC-135E. Along with having thirty percent more power and decreased smoke pollution levels, these aircraft were eighty-five percent quieter.

A second program for replacement of engines, which began in 1982, involved the manufacture of kits to replace existing engines with quieter, more fuel efficient CFM-56 engines. The modified aircraft, designated KC-135R/T, have significantly lower fuel consumption and reduced pollution and noise levels. Performance is significantly enhanced and fuel off-load capability is greatly improved. The aircraft can take off with more fuel, carry it further, and transfer greater amounts to receiving aircraft. By 1999, over 400 KC-135 aircraft had been converted to KC-135R/T configuration.

In 1995, a contract was awarded to increase the versatility of the KC-135R/T tankers by the installation of wingtip mounted hose and drogue refuelling pods. These Mk.32B pods, supplied by Flight Refuelling Ltd., have been installed on forty-five aircraft. This equipment enables the modified tankers to refuel US Navy and NATO aircraft, as well as USAF aircraft using the standard boom and receptacle original equipment.

In 1961, fifteen troop carrier and cargo versions were ordered as the C-135A, powered by the JT-3C turbojet engines. These aircraft are similar to the KC-135 except that they have a larger model 707 type vertical stabilizer, and no refueling capability. In later years, many were upgraded with the TF33 turbofans and wide span tailplanes and redesignated as the C-135E. Thirty C-135B were built equipped with JT-3D/TF33 turbofans and wide span tailplanes. Several of these remain in service in that configuration. The C-135C designator was applied to three ex WC-135B weather reconnaissance aircraft which reverted to transport status. Most other

A KC-135A tanker of the USAF Strategic Air Command. *(Richard J. De Launais)*

CHAPTER ONE

A KC-135E tanker of the USAF Tennessee Air National Guard flies past with the refuelling boom deployed.
(Richard J. De Launais)

C-135B aircraft were converted to various special mission variants.

The C-135C "Speckled Trout" communications aircraft served as an aerial testbed for emerging technology. Developmental tests using this aircraft demonstrated the ability to fly precision approaches using a local area differential GPS system. This modified aircraft has been fitted with a millimetre wave camera and a new radome to test the camera's generation of video images of the forward scene in low visibility conditions. The aircraft gives the Joint Forces Air Component commander a limited ability to plan and control simulated battle while en route to the crisis area.

Early in KC-135 production, a requirement for an Airborne Command Post (ABCP) was identified by the Strategic Air Command (SAC). The concept involved specially equipped aircraft to be airborne at all times in the event that SAC's underground command centre was destroyed or disabled. The first aircraft adapted for this role were seventeen TF33 equipped KC-135B tankers, named "Looking Glass", since they mirrored the ground-based command, control and communications. Operations began on 3 February 1961, and by 1964 the aircraft were redesignated as EC-135 since they were dedicated to the ABCP role. By 1990 the fleet ceased continuous operation but remained on alert twenty-four hours a day.

Eight ex-American Airlines 707-323C aircraft were purchased and after refurbishment were put into service as C-18A crew trainers with new military serial numbers. In 1967, eight ex-C-135A aircraft were converted into EC-135N. Known as A/RIA, for Apollo/Range Instrumented aircraft, they were used in the U.S. Space Program. After completion of the Apollo Program, their designator was changed to ARIA (for Advanced Range Instrumented Aircraft), being used as communication links between space vehicles and the NASA Control Center in Houston.

In 1985, four of these EC-135N aircraft were converted to EC-18B models by incorporation of much of the EC-135N equipment. The EC-18B is recognizable by the large nose-mounted radome, used for telemetry reception, and the HF probe antennas installed at the rear of the wingtips, and the trailing wire antenna package mounted in the belly of the aircraft. Also, two ex-civilian 707-320C aircraft were converted to TC-18E trainers. An additional two ex-civilian 707-320C aircraft were converted to TC-18F trainers for the E-6A Mercury program.

On 25 September 1998, the "Looking Glass" operation was handed over to the U.S. Navy. The mission of

Boeing CC137 (707-347C)

A KC-135R tanker of the USAF on the ramp at CFB Trenton. *(A. Stachiw)*

command, control and communications of the U.S. strategic nuclear forces was assumed by the E-6A Mercury, a long range communication relay airplane designed to communicate with ballistic missile submarines. These were designed to replace the Lockheed EC-130Q TACAMO aircraft, and the first was delivered in 1987. These aircraft were powered by the GE/SNECMA CFM-6 turbofan engines.

A fleet of heavily modified C-135 airframes were operated as aerial test beds under the designations NC-135A, NKC-135A, and NKC-135E. Work performed by these aircraft included refuelling tests with new aircraft types, airborne laser trials, weightless training for astronauts, and programs involving the testing of airborne equipment and space technology.

The RC-135 family of aircraft are dedicated to various strategic missions, detached on a global basis to cover areas requiring intelligence gathering. These included the RC-135U "Combat Sent," RC-135V/W "Rivet Joint" and RC-135S "Cobra Ball" roles.

Three specially equipped 707-153 aircraft, designated VC-137A, were produced in 1959 to transport the President of the United States and other government officials. The first of these VC-137A aircraft flew on 7 April 1959. When the President was on board, any of these were given the call sign "Air Force One." These aircraft were fitted with P&W JT-3C-6 turbojet powerplants, but were retrofitted with P&W JT-3D turbofans in 1963 and redesignated VC-137B. These aircraft were later downgraded to cargo duties and retired in 1998. The most famous of these aircraft, serial number 26000, is currently on display at the U.S. Air Force Museum, Wright Patterson Air Force Base, Ohio.

In 1972, a 707-353B model was added to the fleet, designated VC-137C, serial number 27000. This aircraft served as the fourth presidential aircraft from 1962 to 1972, and was retired in 1998. In 1972, a second 707-353B model was added. This served as the fifth presidential aircraft from 1972 to 1989 and was retired in 2001. The VIP fleet was operated by the 89th Military Airlift Wing based at Andrews Air Force Base, Maryland. This formation was later downgraded to a Group. These aircraft were employed in this role until replaced in 1990 by a variant of the Boeing 747-200, designated VC-25A.

The most dramatic development in the Boeing 707 lineage was the E-3A Sentry AWACS or Airborne Warning and Control System. The aircraft, based on a modified 707-320B airframe, was developed for the USAF Tactical Air Command and Aerospace Defense Command. The AWACS is unmatched in its scope and capability, serving as an all-weather airborne platform for detection and tracking of moving targets at both high and low altitudes. It has high resistance to radar jamming or metallic chaff, provides instant processing of operational information and comprehensive command and control of widespread operations. These unique capabilities are also suited to a variety of civil applications, such as the detection of smuggling activities and the support of counter drug missions.

CHAPTER ONE

In the first part of the program, which was known as "Brassboard," Boeing modified two EC-137D airframes to perform as testbeds for the competing radars and test equipment. Modifications to the airframe included provision for both the operational crew and the AWACS equipment. The AWACS equipment includes a 30 ft. diameter "rotodome" mounted on the aft portion of the fuselage on two pylons. The rotodome houses the surveillance radar antennas, identification friend or foe (IFF), and data link fighter control (TADIL-C) antennas. Other equipment includes beacon interrogators, automatic tracking for both radar and beacon returns, navigation and communication equipment, data processing, identification and presentation equipment and displays, and software systems. These two aircraft were later converted to E-3A, then E-3B standard.

The range and versatility of its airframe allows the aircraft to be deployed anywhere in the world, able to be refueled in the air and carrying its own supply of spares for critical subsystems. As a consequence, the AWACS missions are to a great degree independent of base support. In its tactical role, AWACS serves as an autonomous command and control centre, directing counterair, interdiction, close air support, reconnaissance and airlift missions. Functions include operations as a tactical control centre, airborne direct air support centre, and as an airborne control and reporting centre. In the air defence role, AWACS provides improved survivability for the surveillance, command and control portions of the air defence system with improved radar coverage over both land and water.

In October 1975, engineering test and evaluation began on the first E-3A Sentry. In March 1977, the 552nd Airborne Warning and Control Wing at Tinker AFB, Oklahoma received the first E-3A aircraft. The USAF Air Combat Command as of August 2002 has E-3 based at Tinker AFB, at Elmendorf AFB, Alaska, and at Kadena AB in Japan. Pacific Air Forces has E-3 assigned to the 961st Airborne Air Control Squadron, Kadena AB, Japan, and the 962nd AACS, Elmendorf AFB, Alaska.

Since the inception of the USAF E-3 Sentry AWACS Program, the Canadian Forces have maintained a Canadian Component, both at Tinker AFB, under the 552nd AWAC Wing as well as in Alaska with the 962nd AWACS (later Airborne Air Control Squadron) under the 3rd Wing at Elmendorf AFB. The latter fell under the Alaskan Air Command and later PACAF. On September 22, 1995, USAF E-3A Sentry AWACS, serial no. 77-035 of the 962nd Airborne Air Control Squadron of the 3rd Wing crashed into a thickly wooded area off the end of the runway on takeoff from Elmendorf AFB. The mishap was attributed to the ingestion of Canada geese by the engines. All 24 crew members, including members of the Canadian Component were killed.

The E-3 fleet has been continually modernized to meet its evolving mission requirements. The Boeing Aircraft Company was awarded a contract in May 1987 to begin a long-term improvement program for the AWACS. The biggest effort associated with this integration contract was the full-scale development and integration of an Electronic Support Measures System into the E-3 fleet, which will reduce the risk of attack by detecting signals emitted by both friendly and hostile aircraft and will help identify them. These upgraded aircraft were designated E-3B. Later, some of the upgraded fleet were fitted with CFM-56 powerplants and designated E-3D.

Beginning in 1982, the North Atlantic Treaty Organization (NATO) took delivery of a fleet of eighteen E-3A Sentry AWACS aircraft as well as support equipment and trainers. The NATO aircraft are equipped with the same Pratt & Whitney TF33-PW-100A turbofan engines as those installed in the USAF aircraft (an advanced military version of the JT-3D). As well, Saudi Arabia has purchased a fleet of five E-3A Sentry AWACS aircraft.

Great Britain purchased seven E-3D aircraft, designated as AEW.Mk.1 Sentry for service in their NATO AWACS component. These are equipped with more advanced CFM-56 engines allowing operation at higher altitudes, extending the range of the surveillance radars. France has purchased four aircraft designated E-3F, also equipped with CFM-56 engines. The Armee de l'Air aircraft have had the wingtip refuelling pods installed as well in the recent past.

Another application of the 707 design was Boeing's offer to provide "tanker/transport" aircraft, designated KC-137, to military customers. Retired 707-320C aircraft from the airline inventory would be overhauled, thoroughly inspected, and modernized. Special military avionics would be installed in addition to the commercial instrumentation and avionics. Dual rendezvous radar, weather radar, TACAN, IFF, dual UHF with direction finder were some of the additional enhancements offered. Thrust reverse for the engines was available, and other major modifications included strengthened outer wings and new wing tips. In addition, improved hydraulics and fuel pumps were installed.

Boeing CC137 (707-347C)

There were three optional configurations included in the refuelling package:

1. Either Beech 1080 or Sargent-Fletcher wingtip hose and drogue refuelling stores along with flying boom refuelling station under the aft fuselage with boom operator's station;
2. Either Beech 1080 or Sargent-Fletcher wingtip hose and drogue refueling stores and Sargent-Fletcher centreline hose and drogue installation;
3. Either flying boom refuelling station under the aft fuselage with boom operator's station, or Sargent-Fletcher centreline hose and drogue installation.

Also, the installation of either a probe or receptacle type air-to-air refuelling capability for the tanker aircraft itself was offered. These aircraft still retained the multi-configuration interior arrangements when used as transports, since all additional fuel tank options were installed in the lower fuselage. In addition to sales of the tanker/ transport conversions, there were several VIP conversions of various models of the 707 and 720 aircraft sold to several countries all over the world, as well as cargo/transports.

Earlier, Boeing had begun work on the concept of using the 767 aircraft as a tanker in 1999 by assembling a team to undertake preliminary design development. In 2000, wind tunnel testing took place, and proximity trials were flown from NAS Patuxent River, Maryland using a civilian 767-300ER aircraft. An F/A-18 Hornet, acting as a small category receiver, and later, an S-3 Viking acting as a medium sized receiver were flown in the 767 aircraft's wake to determine the viability of the 767 as a tanker platform. In June 2002, using a 767-200ER, similar testing was done with a C-17A Globemaster III to assess the effect on a large aircraft with a T-tail configuration.

Boeing officially launched the program in March 2001. The aircraft earmarked for the replacement of the KC-135 fleet is the Boeing 767-200ER Tanker/Transport. In July 2001 Italy was the first customer with an order for four 767-200ER Combi aircraft with freight door, powered by GE CF6-80C2 engines. Japan followed in December 2001 with an order for four aircraft. Converted secondhand 767-300ER aircraft are also being considered by the RAF as the next tanker aircraft to replace their fleet of Lockheed L-1011 Tristars, which were converted ex-British Airways passenger liners.

By 2003, the USAF began disposing of surplus KC-135 aircraft. On 23 May 2003 Boeing announced that it had received authorization to build 100 767 refuellers for the USAF. Initially, remaining KC-135A, then KC-135E tankers will be replaced. Eventually, it is foreseen that all KC-135 tankers will be withdrawn from service in favour of the KC-767 aircraft. As well, other versions utilizing the 707 platform are potential candidates for replacement with a 767 platform aircraft. Other air forces operating 707 Tanker/Transports will eventually become potential customers as their aircraft reach retirement age.

BOEING 707 COMMERCIAL VARIANTS

For the commercial market, Boeing mounted a vigorous sales campaign for the Model 367-80, approaching all major airlines. The Douglas Aircraft Company had now entered the race with their DC-8 design, as had Convair with Model 880 and Model 990 jet transports. The airlines began to warm to the now proven jet transport designs. The 707 production aircraft was modified to win the commercial orders in reaction to the DC-8 proposal. The fuselage was widened and lengthened slightly, and the gross weight increased.

On 16 October 1955 the prototype was flown on a record-breaking return transcontinental flight in eight hours by Tex Johnston. In the meantime, on 13 October 1955 the first order for the 707 had been placed by Pan American Airways for twenty aircraft. Orders began to mount as the original hesitance of the airlines vanished in light of the aircraft's achievements. On 28 October 1957 the first production aircraft, designated 707-121, registered N707PA of Pan American Airways was rolled out. After undergoing the required CAA (predecessor of the FAA) flight test program, the aircraft was issued a type certificate on 23 September 1958. The aircraft entered service with Pan American Airways on 26 October when it inaugurated New York to Paris trans-Atlantic service with 111 passengers aboard. The first U.S. domestic service was on the Miami to New York route by National Airlines using leased Pan American aircraft. Transcontinental service was started by American Airlines with their 707-123 model aircraft on 25 January 1959.

The 707-120 series closely approximated the original 367-80 prototype Stratoliner, although it was made slightly larger with a higher gross weight as well as uprated Pratt & Whitney JT-3 engines. A special version, the 707-138, having a 10 ft. shorter fuselage, was

CHAPTER ONE

Boeing 707 N7070T CFM-56 Test demonstrator aircraft. *(Boeing Aircraft Co. Neg. No. C49591)*

produced for Quantas Empire Airways of Australia. Braniff International Airways of the United States ordered five of a higher powered version designated 707-227, powered by the Pratt & Whitney JT-4 engine. Dimensionally the same as the -120 series, the -220 series were better suited for the routes served by Braniff. A medium range version, designated Model 720 was also produced, featuring both turbojet and turbofan powerplants. This variant was generally similar to the 707-120 series. The -300 and -400 Intercontinental series aircraft had a substantial increase in gross weight accompanied by a longer fuselage and a larger wing and tailplane. As the name suggested, this was the long range version, capable of carrying more passengers over much greater distances.

With the advent of the turbofan or bypass engine, with its greatly increased power and economy, the 707 was equipped with these powerplants, and immediately displayed improved performance. With the turbofan engines, the 707-120 series was redesignated 707-120B, and the 707-300 series became the 707-300B. The first model featuring the bypass engine was the -400 version equipped with the Rolls Royce Model 508 Conway engine. This version served with Lufthansa and Cunard-Eagle as the model 707-436, BOAC (now British Airways) and Air India as the 707-437, Varig as the 707-445, and with El Al as the Model 707-458. With the introduction of the Pratt & Whitney JT-3D turbofan engines, the demand for this variant ceased. The -300 series also introduced new refined wingtips, improved high lift flaps, and other aerodynamic enhancements which conferred improvements to the aircraft's flight characteristics and overall performance. Very long range routes now became possible.

A further development was the introduction of a large cargo door on the forward port side of the fuselage. Models so equipped were given a "C" suffix in their designator. This installation, along with a strengthened floor and landing gear, became the basis for the 707-300C variant, a convertible cargo-passenger carrying aircraft which was otherwise similar to the 707-300B series. A further development resulted in the 707-320C variant, with built-in convertibility for carrying large troop, cargo, or combination loads over intercontinental stages.

As part of the improvement and development of the 707 family, in cooperation with General Electric and SNECMA of France, a 707-700 model was developed equipped with the CFM56 series of large turbofan engines. Boeing installed the CFM56 engines in a test and demonstrator aircraft, registered N7070T. This conversion was undertaken in a large number of civilian 707 aircraft. The improvement in performance and economy greatly enhanced the capabilities of the converted aircraft.

In retrospect, the 707 family of aircraft must rank as one of the most significant and successful aircraft designs of all time. Although now replaced in frontline service with the airlines, it was a frontrunner in changing the means of international travel. When the 707 production line closed at the end of May, 1991, some 1,010 examples of all versions of the commercial aircraft had been produced, as well as 820 of the Model 717, or KC-135 and C-135 military variants.

CHAPTER TWO
The CC137 in Canadian Service

The Boeing CC137 fleet lined up on the hardstand at CFB Trenton.
(Courtesy of the Department of National Defence [DND])

CHAPTER TWO

The Canadair CC106 Yukon aircraft, the predecessor of the Boeing CC137 in Air Transport Command.
(DND, Neg. No. PL-13827-1)

Artist's impression of Boeing C-135/707 in RCAF markings.
(Andrew Cline)

Boeing CC137 (707-347C)

During the 1960s, the long range heavy lift requirements of the Royal Canadian Air Force were filled by the Canadair CC106 Yukon, a military version of the Canadair CL-44D-6 transport. This aircraft was an adaptation of the Bristol Britannia turboprop airliner which had revolutionized commercial air travel in the 1950s. There were twelve aircraft in the Yukon fleet. Ten were operated by 437 Transport Squadron from their base at RCAF Station Trenton, Ontario, and two by 412 VIP Squadron based at RCAF Station Uplands near Ottawa..

In the late 1960s, the Canadian government expressed interest in purchasing a fleet of KC-135 aircraft to replace the CC106 Yukon fleet. In addition to the transport role, these aircraft would have fulfilled the air-to-air refuelling requirements in support of the CF-5 Freedom Fighter operations projected by Mobile Command. As it turned out, the KC-135 production line at the Boeing Aircraft Company had closed, and none were available from the USAF inventory of over 700 aircraft.

Negotiations were then carried on with the Lockheed Aircraft Corporation for the purchase of the C-141A Starlifter aircraft to replace the Yukon fleet. This large cargo transport featured a rear loading/unloading ramp accessed through large clamshell doors under the aft fuselage. These doors could be opened in flight for drops of paratroops or equipment by parachute, and the aircraft could be equipped for inflight refuelling of fighter aircraft, and had an installation enabling it to be refuelled in the air. As it turned out, the availability of the aircraft was conditional on reaching a decision by a certain date to keep the production line open. The production of the aircraft for the USAF was reaching an end, and the aircraft, if the Canadian government could reach a decision, would be added to the end of the production line. Because at this time cutbacks in defence funding and a shift in defence policy were in progress, the decision was not reached in time, and the production line was shut down. Lockheed then scrapped the tooling for the aircraft, rendering any further negotiations pointless.

Artist's impression of Lockheed C-141 Starlifter in RCAF Markings.
(Andrew Cline)

CHAPTER TWO

Lockheed C-141B Starlifter heavy transport aircraft of the USAF. An earlier version, the C-141A was a contender for the heavy transport role requirements of the Canadian Forces.
(A. Stachiw)

In 1968, the West German Luftwaffe had purchased four 707-307C convertible cargo/ passenger aircraft from Boeing. With no prospect of purchasing any dedicated military heavy lift jet transport, the Canadian government approached the Boeing Aircraft Company with a similar requirement in mind, and was informed of the availability of four 707-347C convertible cargo/passenger aircraft which could be delivered in short order. The order had originally been placed by Western Airlines, and was well advanced on the production line.

After the signing of the contract, which specified the conversion of two of these aircraft to a tanker/transport configuration at a later date, acceptance testing by a crew from 448 Test Squadron of the Aerospace Engineering and Test Establishment and crew training was conducted at the Boeing Aircraft Company facilities in Seattle, Washington. The first four aircraft were delivered to CFB Trenton on 10 April 1970 with an impressive arrival ceremony. The fifth was delivered 11 May 1971 under a different agreement.

All five aircraft were taken on strength by 437 Transport Squadron, based at CFB Trenton, in Air Transport Command in the long range heavy transport role. Compared to the CC106 Yukon transports, the CC137 aircraft could carry a substantially larger load over far greater distances. As a result, the capabilities of Air Transport Command (later Air Transport Group) were greatly increased. There were, however, certain disadvantages compared to the Yukon. The decrease in fleet size affected operational capability, which became dependent on maintenance scheduling or accident. As well, the aircraft was restricted to the fewer airfields able to support the CC137 compared to the CC106 Yukon. Nevertheless, the gain in Air Transport Group's transport capability was substantial.

The aircraft were flown on a regularly scheduled route between Air Movements Units in Canada, to Gatwick in the U.K., and to CFB Lahr in the Federal Republic of Germany. One flight continued on to Egypt to support the Canadian United Nations Expeditionary Force Detachment in the Middle East. Twice a year, the Canadian Battalion on UN duty in Cyprus was rotated, and troop lifts were carried out as a part of various exercises. Heavy lift was also carried out on "Operation Boxtop," the resupply of Northern bases, the freight being carried as far as the USAF base at Thule, Greenland, where it was then forwarded by Canadian Forces CC130 Hercules aircraft. The cross-Canada flights were discontinued in 1991 when the service was contracted out to civilian carriers.

The CC137 aircraft were also employed in the VIP role, providing transport for the Prime Minister as well as other government officials to all parts of the world. The first such tasking occurred soon after the aircraft

Boeing CC137 (707-347C)

Her Majesty Queen Elizabeth II boards a CC137 aircraft at the conclusion of a state visit to Canada. *(DND)*

entered service with 437(T) Squadron when Prime Minister Trudeau toured Expo 70 at Osaka, Japan, and the Pacific region from 10 May to 29 May 1970. Soviet Premier Alexi Kosygin toured Canada from 22–24 October 1971, transported by CC137. In 1973, Prime Minister and Mrs. Trudeau were carried by the 437(T) Squadron VIP Flight on their visit to the People's Republic of China. As well, during royal visits the CC137, with a suitable interior arrangement, provided transport for the Queen and Prince Philip, or other visiting dignitaries. This was also the case when Pope John Paul II visited Canada in 1984.

The addition of the air-to-air refueling capability added a whole new dimension to Transport Group's operations. The Canadian Forces were the first customer for the tanker/transport conversion. In 1971 and 1972, aircraft serial numbers 13703 and 13704 were returned to the Boeing plant to be retrofitted with Beech 1080 aerial refuelling kits. The installation in 13703 had the basic refuelling equipment installed by 19 May 1972, and 13704 by October 1972.

Qualification training of the CF-5 pilots from AETE, 433 ETAC, and 434 TACF(OT) Squadrons began in November 1972. To qualify, each pilot participated in five dry contacts, twenty wet contacts, and one night contact. By the end of January, 1973 pilots from all units had qualified. By June 1973 the tanker force was operational. This enabled the deployment of CF-5 Freedom Fighters to Norway to fulfill the commitment of the Canadian Forces to the defence of the Northern Flank of NATO. The first of many such deployments, with two CC137 tankers and four CF-5As from each of 433 ETAC and 434 TAC(F) Squadrons took place on 9 June 1973 in Operation Long Leap I, to the Norwegian Base at Andoya. The flight, involving five aerial refuellings, took approximately six hours, and covered a distance of 3,150 miles.

On 18 June 1979, with a CC137 tanker, four CF-5As from 434 TACF(OT) Squadron orbited the North Pole in Operation Ice Cap, a show of Canadian sovereignty. In Exercise Rhine Hornet, from 17–19 May 1984, the first of the deployments of CF188 Hornet fighters to CFB

CHAPTER TWO

Baden-Solingen in Germany was carried out with CC137 refuellers escorting the formations. All subsequent CF-188 flights to 1 CAG were accomplished non-stop with air-to-air refueling by the CC137 tankers. During the buildup of Coalition Forces for Operation Desert Storm following the invasion by Iraq of Kuwait, the CF188 Hornet fighters of 409 Tac(F) Squadron were deployed to the Canada Dry One Base at Doha, Qatar supported by the CC137 refuellers. A second deployment from Baden by 439 Tac(F) Squadron was accomplished later. The CC137 transport aircraft of 437(T) Squadron also supported the Canadian contingent during their service in the Gulf area. There was an interesting occurrence involving a CC137 tanker during the deployment. A US Navy F-14 Tomcat fighter in imminent danger of running out of fuel was tanked up by a CC137. The refuelling was accomplished although the clearance between the tail of the CC137 and the fighter was minimal. The crew of the Tomcat would have had to eject and the aircraft would have been lost were it not for the timely intervention of the Canadian tanker.

Following the Gulf War, beginning in 1991 and the end of 1992 the three fighter squadrons based at CFB Baden were disbanded. In 1994 in Operation Rhine Prosit, the CC137 tankers supported the return of the CF188 Hornet aircraft to Canada. Later on, the CC137s

8 Wing groundcrew load medical supplies aboard 13705 on 10 May 1994 at CFB Trenton for a flight to Copenhagen, Denmark, as part of Operation Boreal IV. The Boreal operation ran in four separate cases, staging from various bases with both Boeing CC137 and Lockheed CC130 Hercules aircraft providing airlift of Red Cross medical supplies and foodstuffs to cities in Eastern Europe and the former Soviet Union. 437 Squadron became the first western unit to operate into Russian airspace during Operation Boreal I.

(Andrew Cline)

Boeing CC137 (707-347C)

Airbus Industrie (A310) CC150 Polaris aircraft on the ramp at CFB Trenton. The Polaris replaced the Boeing CC137 in the heavy lift role in the CF's Air Transport Group.
(Richard J. De Launais)

were used to support the deployment of CF188 Hornets to Turkey to enforce the No-Fly zone over Northern Iraq.

The CC137 fleet was also employed in a humanitarian role. In 1981, in Operation Magnet II which took place between 26 July and 26 August, 2,136 Vietnamese "Boat People" were carried from Hong Kong to their new homes in Canada. Some 212 passengers were carried in each of eleven flights. The 17,400 mile return flight from CFB Trenton to Hong Kong was staged through Elmendorf Air Base in Alaska and Tokyo, Japan, and took a total of thirty-six hours. A similar evacuation of Pakistani refugees recorded a total of 241 people carried on one flight. Other operations involved the transport of emergency food relief to Somalia and the Sudan, as well as other such relief flights under United Nations auspices.

A CC137 aircraft was also tested with a palletized command module in an attempt to configure it as an Airborne Command Post. Technical problems proved the concept was not feasible. The dedication of an aircraft to use exclusively as an ACP could not be justified considering the high priorities associated with the existing multiple taskings already assigned to the fleet. It soon became apparent that the five-aircraft fleet was inadequate for the various roles that were being assigned, especially the air-to-air refuelling taskings assigned to the two tanker aircraft, and the purchase of two more CC137 aircraft was requested in 1977. The purchase of another tanker was requested in 1986, with Senate approval, and the 1987 White Paper on Defence recommended the purchase of additional transport aircraft, including CC137s, but no action was taken.

Several configurations were developed for the aircraft to perform these various duties:

1. PASSENGER. 170 to 212 seated passengers could normally be carried with different seat spacings, but as many as 241 were carried in an emergency evacuation from Pakistan.

2. VIP. A stateroom for heads of state seating 8 with accommodation for 115 seats aft of the stateroom. Alternately, a mini capsule for 6 senior officials with high density accommodation for 155 seats aft.

3. MIXED CONFIGURATION. Three pallets of cargo forward weighing 25,000 lbs/42,000 kg with 112 seats aft.

4. CARGO. Up to 90,000 lbs./42,000 kg. Range over 2500 nautical miles/4000 km.

5. MEDEVAC. 60 litters plus 45 seats for support personnel.

CHAPTER TWO

6. AIR REFUELLING. Along with the fuel itself, 50 passengers and 25,000 lbs/12,500 kg of support equipment.

In 1977, the projected retirement of the CC137 fleet was set for 1986, and at one time was extended as far as 2010. However, the decision to re-engine and overhaul the aircraft was cancelled in favour of replacing them with a fleet of Airbus Industrie A-310 aircraft. These aircraft, which entered service with the Canadian Forces as the CC150 Polaris, were originally purchased by Wardair, and subsequently had been taken over by Canadian Airlines and then sold off. The fleet had been equipped with long range fuel tanks, which made them suitable for the Canadian Forces requirement. The CC150 Polaris supplemented and then replaced the CC137 fleet. The last CC137 aircraft, the two tankers 13703 and 13704, were retired in 1997. At the time of writing, two of the CC150 aircraft are scheduled to have an air-to-air refuelling system installed in conjunction with a similar requirement issued by the German Luftwaffe.

The five aircraft in the CC137 fleet flew a total of 191,154 hours, with 13702 having the highest total at 38,762 hours in its log book. The estimated mileage flown was 80,793,000 miles. Although the selection of the CC137 for the heavy transport role was a compromise (since a suitable military aircraft was not available), it performed well throughout its service life. Three of the aircraft, after having been declared surplus, were refurbished and entered service with the US Military in the Joint Surveillance Target Attack Radar System Program (J-STARS).

CC137 FLEET STATISTICS

S/N	C/N	TOS	Del Date	SOS	Prev. Reg'n	New Reg'n	Date	Comments
13701	20315	70.2.24	70.2.25	93.8.30	N1506W		94.1.19	Sold to American International Airways, Ypsilanti, Michigan, USA
							94.	Sold to Race Aviation, Miami, Florida, USA
13702	20316	70.2.24	70.2.18	93.3.2	N1507W		93.12.17	Sold to Omega Air, Ireland
						PT-TCU	94.7.1 to 96.12	Leased to Transbrasil Airlines
						EL-AKT	95.5	Omega Air
						95-0123	95.10.	Purchased for USAF/US Army Joint Surveillance Target Attack Radar System (J-STARS) Program before conversion by Grumman Aerospace
						96-0043	01.5.	Converted to E-8B, reserialled.
13703	20317	70.2.24	70.3.2	97.4.1	N1508W		97.4.17	Purchased for J-STARS Program
						97-0200		E-8B
13704	20318	70.2.24	70.3.10	97.4.1	N1509W		97.4.17	Purchased for J-STARS Program
						97-0201		E-8B
13705	20319	71.3.24	71.3.23	95.4.29	N1510W		95.6.23	Purchased for J-STARS Program
						96-0042		E-8B

Note: After unification of the Canadian Armed Forces, which was initiated in 1965, the RCAF system of aircraft type designation and serial numbering was replaced, in 1972, by a CTS Control Number (Chief of Technical Services), which contained as the prefix the numerical part of the CTS control number, followed by a sequential tail number. In this system, the 707-347C was assigned the designator CC137, while Boeing 707 remained the popular name. In the CC137 fleet, the aircraft were assigned the serial range 13701-13705.

Boeing CC137 (707-347C)

Boeing E-8C Joint Surveillance Target Attack Radar System (J-STARS) 92-3290. 12 ACCS, 93rd ACW (first squadron with aircraft at that time) Robins AFB, GA. Shown here at USAF 50th Anniversary Golden Air Tattoo, Nellis AFB, NV April 24, 1997. Although not an ex-CAF aircraft, this image clearly illustrates the large canoe fairing housing the ground surveillance radar, the backbone of the J-STARS system.

(Andrew Cline)

CHAPTER THREE
Aircraft Description and Drawings

Boeing CC137 13703 on the ramp at CFB Trenton. *(A. Stachiw)*

BOEING CC137
Boeing designator 707-347C, CTS Control Number CC137

Description: High speed jet transport operating in the heavy strategic transport role, as a VIP transport, and as an inflight refuelling tanker in support of tactical fighter operations.

Powerplant: Four Pratt & Whitney JT3D-7 turbofan engines mounted on underwing pylons 19,000 lbs. (8607 kg.) thrust

Dimensions:
- Wingspan 145 ft 9 in (44.45 m)
- Height 42 ft 6 in (12.95 m)
- Length 152 ft 11 in (46.68 m)
- Wing Area 3010 ft^2 (279.74 m^2)

Weights: Basic: 140,000 lbs. (63,569 kg.)
Max Permissible Takeoff Weight: 333,600 lbs. (151,454.4 kg.)
Total Fuel Weight: 151,500 lbs. (33,700.44 kg.)

Performance: Maximum level speed 627 mph (1010 kph)
Maximum Cruising Speed 600 mph (965.58 kph) at 25,000 ft. (7620 m.)
Economical Cruising Speed 550 mph (886 kph)
Stalling speed with flaps down at max. landing weight 121 mph (195 kph)
Rate of climb at sea level 2940 fpm (896 mpm)
Service Ceiling 38,500 ft. (11,735 m.)

Range: 6,000 miles (9655.8 kms)

Systems: Two externally mounted Beech Model 1080 refuelling pods (aircraft 13703, 13704 only)

Front view of CC137 aircraft. *(A. Stachiw)*

CHAPTER THREE

Three-quarter front port side view of CC137 aircraft. *(A. Stachiw)*

Port side view of CC137 aircraft. Note the cabin entry doors, main cargo door, and emergency escape hatches. *(A. Stachiw)*

Three-quarter rear port side view of CC137 aircraft. *(A. Stachiw)*

Boeing CC137 (707-347C)

Rear view of CC137 aircraft. *(A. Stachiw)*

Three-quarter rear starboard side view of CC137 aircraft. *(A. Stachiw)*

Starboard side view of CC137 aircraft. Note the galley and cargo doors, and emergency escape hatches. *(A. Stachiw)*

CHAPTER THREE

Three-quarter front starboard side view of CC137 aircraft. *(A. Stachiw)*

The CC137 aircraft has a double lobed fuselage common to all variants of the 707 family, and is divided into three major sections: the control cabin, the main cabin and the tail compartment. The fuselage is an all-metal semi-monocoque fail-safe structure utilizing longitudinal hat section stringers and clad skin. The shell is stiffened circumferentially by bulkheads and "Z" or web and extruded section frames. Production breaks occur at Fuselage Stations 360 and 1440 (see Drawing Page 52).

The semi-monocoque structure is considered a complete torque box throughout its length, all cutouts for doors, service access openings and windows having adequate local reinforcement. The skinning carrying hoop tension in addition to body bending loads are generally clad aluminum and magnesium. The fuselage skin is installed with circumferential butt joints and longitudinal lap joints and is flush riveted. The fuselage bending that is carried in a triangular torque box that runs under the wing, is transferred by shear to the wing lower surface. Wing to fuselage attachment structure consists of terminal fittings at body bulkheads 600K and 820. The upper surface of the wing is attached to the fuselage through a shear joint between upper rib chord WBL-6 and the fuselage skin.

The nose landing gear retracts forward into the underside of the aircraft nose. Bulkheads at Fuselage Stations 259.5, 312 and 360 support the nose wheel structure and the nose landing gear and carry these loads into the monocoque structure. The main landing gear trucks retract inwards into the wing centre section.

The sides of the fuselage are cut away from stringers S18a to S29 between bulkheads at Fuselage Stations 820 to 960 to allow the main landing gear to be retracted inside the lower lobe of the fuselage. Vertical shear is carried in this area through a keel beam which connects the pressure deck at WL 202 to stringer S29 at the bottom of the fuselage. Main gear side loads in the side struts are carried to the monocoque structure through forged floor beams at Fuselage Stations 880 and 890.

The floor structure, consisting of beams, intercostals and panels, is supported through the fuselage frames and side attachments. All floor and pressure loads are distributed into the monocoque structure. The main fuselage pressure bulkheads are at Fuselage Stations 178 and 1440 with intermediate bulkheads at Fuselage Stations 259.5, 360, 600K, 820, and 060. The entire shell is pressurized from Fuselage Stations 178 to 1440 except within the nose gear wheel well and centre wing main landing gear bays. The nose radome extends forward of Fuselage Station 178. Two pressure seals, forward and aft, are installed which prevent the cabin pressurizing air from escaping through the gaps between the centre wing section and the adjacent fuselage bulkheads. A vapour barrier isolates the gap between the centre wing rear spar and the forward bulkhead of the main wheel well from the main wheel well area and the air conditioning equipment bays.

The fuselage structure combined both fail-safe abilities and a long fatigue life. The design provided alternative load paths so that should one member fail the load could be safely taken by adjoining members. Where loads have been taken by a single member, such as the pilot's window frame centre post, the member consists of at least two pieces so that a crack will be initially confined to half of the member. The control of the crack growth in the fuselage structure is accomplished by using materials with slow crack propagation rate, and by providing tear stoppers in the critical structural areas.

The control cabin has four fixed windows consisting of two glass panes laminated to either side of a vinyl core. They are installed by mechanical fasteners and pressure sealed on installation by means of sealant between the surfaces of the windows and the frames. There is a sliding window adjacent to both pilot and copilot, mounted on tracks, which can be rolled back to permit ventilation and communication during ground handling manoeuvres. All windows are equipped with electrical anti-icing and defogging.

The passenger windows are regularly spaced between the frames at twenty-inch increments in those areas of the cabin where passenger seating is provided. The only variation in spacing occurred on the main cargo door, where the first and last of the windows are respaced to accommodate the door structure. They consist of acrylic outer, centre and inner panels. Breather holes in the centre panes permit enough airflow to prevent fogging. The outer panel is rectangular with rounded corners, with a peripheral silicone rubber seal and is shaped to the fuselage contour.

There are two main doors to the passenger cabin located on the port side at Fuselage Stations 312 and 340. They are similar in structure, operating mechanism and operation, but are not interchangeable. They are of the inward-outward opening plug type and can be opened or closed from inside or outside of the aircraft by a centrally located, manually operated handle. Both have a circular double pane window located above the door handle and are supported at the forward edge by an upper and lower hinge assembly.

On the starboard side of the aircraft at Fuselage Stations 420 and 1295, there are forward and aft galley doors permitting access to two galley stations. These, as well, are of the inward-outward opening plug type, and are similar in structure, operating mechanism and operation to the main cabin doors.

There are six emergency escape hatches, three on each side of the fuselage, at Fuselage Stations 678.95,

View of ground start unit and towable airstair in position at the main cabin door. *(A. Stachiw)*

CHAPTER THREE

Port side of forward fuselage showing the main cargo door. Note the modified window spacing at each end of the cargo door.
(A. Stachiw)

758.95, and 978.95. As well, the copilot's sliding window can be opened from outside the aircraft and used as an emergency escape hatch.

The 91 in. x 134 in. (2.31 m. x 3.4 m.) main cargo door is located on the upper port side of the forward fuselage between Fuselage Stations 483 and 600+17, with the lower edge at the level of the cabin floor. It hinges upward and outward and is hydraulically operated. The upper edge is attached to the fuselage by hinge sections located on a fuselage stringer. The structure consists of an alclad pressure web forming the external surface reinforced by circumferential and longitudinal frames. The door is sealed by a continuous pressure seal around the periphery which prevents outward leakage of cabin pressure air and inward weather leakage. Two rectangular openings near the lower corners of the door are closed by inward hinging pressure doors which release any residual cabin pressure before the main door is opened. The cargo door is held in the open position by a strut which can be installed at the forward edge of the door and is held in place by a fitting in the door at the top end and a receptacle in the door frame at the lower end.

On the lower starboard side of the aircraft are cargo doors providing access to the two underfloor cargo compartments. These are located at Fuselage Stations 530, 1040, and 1200. They are similar in structure, operating mechanism and operation. They are of the inward-outward opening plug type and can be opened or closed from inside or outside of the aircraft by a centrally located, manually operated handle. (See the fuselage station diagram and aircraft walkaround photographs for these features, page 52, pages 26-29)

The vertical stabilizer is a fixed auxiliary airfoil surface which gives directional stability to the aircraft and reduces the yawing tendencies about the vertical axis. It is attached to the fuselage by fittings at Fuselage Stations 1440 and 1507. There is no structural tie between the vertical stabilizer skin and fuselage. Torsion on the fin is reacted by side couple loads at Fuselage Stations 1440 and 1507. The HF probe and Loran antennae are positioned on the tip of the stabilizer. The stabilizer and rudder may be folded to the right and may be removed from the aircraft as a unit or the rudder may be removed independently after the folding operation.

Boeing CC137 (707-347C)

Port side view of tailplane.
(A. Stachiw)

Starboard side view of tailplane.
(A. Stachiw)

CHAPTER THREE

The leading edge of the stabilizer is detachable and provides access to the internal structure. The CC137 is not equipped with a dorsal fin, which had been installed on earlier model 707 aircraft.

The vertical stabilizer is of two spar construction, although the front spar web does not extend beyond Fin Station 111.65, and there is no other spanwise stiffening. The contour of the airfoil and torsional strength are maintained by ribs spaced at approximately nine inches. The bending moment and beam shear are carried by the spars and local effective skin. The torsion is reacted by torsional shear in the skin and rear spar web.

The horizontal stabilizer assembly consists of left and right sections attached to a centre torque box located within the aft fuselage. The stabilizer is pivoted on two self aligning bushing type hinge joints attached to a heavy bulkhead and the angle of attack is adjusted by means of an electrically driven or manually operated ball nut and jackscrew attached to the forward side of the centre section torque box. All vertical load distributions on the vertical stabilizer react at the above mentioned three attachment points. The leading edges and tips are removable. A rubber aerodynamic seal fills the gap between the left and right sections of the stabilizer assembly and the fuselage. A brush seal integral with the stabilizer fairing and a sliding plate seal are located respectively at points where the front and rear spars enter the fuselage.

The front and rear spars and the stabilizer skin form a box beam which is the main structural member. The outboard panel is of a two spar construction, the front spar web extending to Stabilizer Station 11.55 only. The spars provide the only spanwise stiffness except for the trailing edge beam at 75 percent chord. Airfoil contour and torsional strength are maintained by ribs at nine inch spacing. The bending moment and beam shear are carried by the spars and local effective skin. The stabilizer torsion is reacted by torsional shear in the skin and rear spar web. Attachment of the outboard panels and centre section is at the front and rear spar only, with no structural tie between the outboard panel skin and centre section.

The wing is a cantilevered box beam, tapered in both planform and depth from root to tip, and swept back at an angle of 350 at quarter chord. The complete wing consists of the main wing, outboard wing assemblies, and the wing tips. The main wing includes both the inboard wing assemblies and the wing centre section which is the same width as, and fits into the lower fuselage.

The wing primary structure is a box beam consisting of two spars, closely spaced inspar ribs, and the longitudinally stiffened skins. In the wing centre section, the ribs are replaced by full depth spanwise beams. The rear spar carries greater loads than the front spar due to the swept wing configuration and is of heavier construction. At two places along the rear spar the angle of sweep is increased slightly; once near the outboard end of the inboard spoiler and again just outboard of the outboard nacelle strut. This latter point of change in sweep is the production break at which the outboard wing assembly can be removed if necessary. The outer removable part of the wing, the wing tip, can be removed from a line perpendicular to the rear spar immediately outboard of the outboard aileron.

The primary structure of the wing box beam also serves as an integral fuel tank. Intermediate ribs act as baffles, the fuel being allowed to circulate through the spaces between the ribs and skin left by the depth of the stringers. Tank end ribs are full depth and divide the wing into left and right centre, inboard, outboard, and reserve fuel tanks. Fuel tanks in the wing centre section are of the conventional bladder cell type, interconnected to the root rib to the left and right centre integral tanks. Access panels are provided along the upper surface of the wing for inspection of the integral tanks. Part of the structure in both left and right wings acts as a dry bay in which the fueling station is located.

Because of the long chordal distance between the spars, the ribs are closely spaced. Most of the ribs have non-perforated webs which are perpendicular to the rear spar with extruded vertical stiffeners to break down the rib panel sizes. Inboard of the inboard nacelle, the rib alignment changes progressively until it is parallel to the aircraft centreline at the main landing gear rib. All of the ribs inboard of the inboard nacelle, except those forming tank ends, have large rectangular cutouts at approximately mid-chord which are spanned by vertical stiffeners. In general the wing ribs have a peripheral gap the depth of the stringers between the rib chords and the wing skin. The exceptions to this are the tank end ribs, engine nacelle ribs, and the landing gear ribs.

Lightning strike laminated armour panels are installed on each upper and lower wing surfaces between the front and rear spars from Wing Stations 939.312 to 959.312. Tapered external stainless steel straps are installed on the upper wing skin just aft of the rear spar at rear spar Wing Stations 211 and 232.

Boeing CC137 (707-347C)

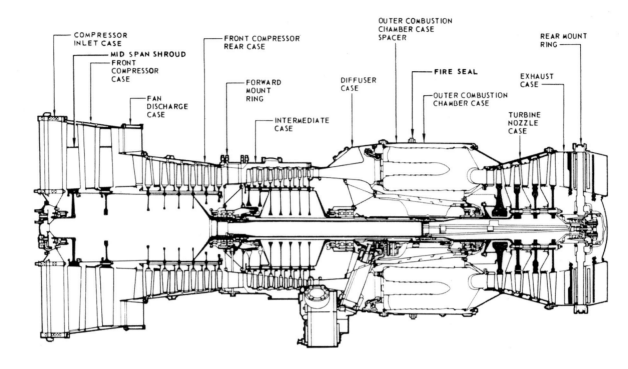

Typical internal arrangement of JTD3-7 series turbofan engine. *(DND)*

Special wing ribs at the nacelle struts distribute engine loads to the wing. These ribs, being parallel to the aircraft centreline, intersect or cut across the normal (perpendicular to rear spar) ribs. Engine nacelle struts connect to faired-in forgings on top and bottom exterior surfaces of the wing. These forgings are bolted, through the skin, to the strengthened wing ribs.

The aircraft is equipped with four Pratt & Whitney JT3D-7 (TF33) twin spool axial flow turbofan engines. Each power plant assembly consists of a turbofan engine, necessary accessory components and auxiliary components. The power plant systems are engine controls, air bleed, engine oil, engine indicating, engine vibration indicating, engine fuel, starting, ignition and reverse thrust.

The engine control system consists of switches and levers necessary to start the engines and control their power output. Engine starts are controlled from the control cabin through engine start control switches and engine start levers, the power output being controlled by the position of the engine thrust levers. An additional handle accompanies each engine thrust lever for actuating thrust reversers.

The engine indicating system consists of instruments necessary for normal control and operation of the engines, for checking engine mechanical condition and for checking and adjusting engine thrust output. The following instruments are located on the pilots' centre panel: engine pressure ratio indicators: N1 low pressure ratio tachometers, engine exhaust temperature indicators, and fuel flow indicators. N2 high pressure rotor tachometers are on the flight engineer's lower panel.

The engines are supported individually in strut mounted nacelles beneath the wings, increasing flight safety and facilitating maintenance, and are attached to the strut at three support fittings designed to allow for thermal expansion of the engine. Hinged cowl sections further contribute to ease of maintenance. Each engine is equipped with a fan thrust reverser and an aft thrust reverser attached at the turbine exhaust case. The main operating accessories attached to the engines are starters, hydraulic pumps (engines 2 and 3), the a/c generators,

CHAPTER THREE

constant speed drive and the turbo compressors (engines 2, 3 and 4).

The engine is a continuous flow gas turbofan consisting of two axial flow compressors in series, a can-annular combustion chamber with eight circumferentially located burner cans, and four impulse reaction turbine wheels in series. The compressor section consists of an eight stage N1 low pressure rotor assembly, and a seven stage N2 high pressure rotor assembly on separate concentric shafts.

The first two front compressor stages are considerably larger in diameter and provide air for two separate streams. The inner stream travels through the engine and the outer stream is ducted to the air nozzle outside of the engine. The fan feature comprises ducting the air stream in the outer periphery of the first two front compressor stages outside of the engine and providing a propulsive force by expanding it through a jet nozzle in the same manner as at the tailpipe, except that the process occurs at a lower temperature. Of the total thrust available from each engine, 41 percent is generated by the primary turbojet engine, while 59 percent is generated by the fan operation.

No.1 engine pod, port outer. Note the absence of the turbo compressor air intake on this pod.
(A. Stachiw)

Boeing CC137 (707-347C)

No.2 engine pod, port inner.
(A. Stachiw)

Port wing and engine pods looking inboard. Note the leading edge slats and trailing edge flaps.
(A. Stachiw)

CHAPTER THREE

No.3 engine pod, starboard inner. *(A. Stachiw)*

No.4 engine pod, starboard outer. *(A. Stachiw)*

Boeing CC137 (707-347C)

View looking inboard of starboard wing and engine pods. Note the landing / taxi lights in the leading edge of the wing outboard of the fuselage.
(A. Stachiw)

Both high and low pressure air bled from the engine case is used to drive pneumatically driven accessories pressurization, and thermal anti-icing. The starter, constant speed drive, and hydraulic pump are attached to the accessory gear box which is driven by the high pressure rotor assembly through a gear train and drive shaft assembly. The fuel pump, fuel control unit and engine oil pump are part of the basic engine assembly and are also driven by the accessory gear box. The high pressure bleed system provides high pressure, high temperature air from the sixteenth stage of the N2 compressor to drive the turbocompressors and provides anti-icing to the turbocompressor and turbocompressor inlets on engines 2, 3 and 4, pressurizes the hydraulic reservoir in the left hand main wheel well, supplies air to the fuel heater, operates thrust reversers, and provides potable water tank system pressure. The low pressure bleed system supplies relatively low pressure medium temperature air from the ninth stage of the N1 compressor for cabin auxiliary air conditioning and pressurization and thermal anti-icing of the wing.

Each power plant has an integral engine oil system, an integral constant speed drive oil system and, on power plants No.2, 3, and 4, an integral turbocompressor oil system. The engine oil system is a high pressure design consisting of a pressure system, scavenge system, and a breather system. The engine oil tank, mounted on the right side of each engine, has a capacity of 6.0 U.S. gallons and stores and de-aerates the oil. Oil temperature, oil pressure and oil quantity indicators are mounted on the flight engineer's panel.

The engine fuel system delivers fuel from tanks in the wings by way of fuel tank boost pumps to the engines at pressures and flow rates as needed to obtain the thrust output required. Thrust lever position, burner pressure and N2 compressor RPM are the input signals to the fuel control unit. These signals are interpreted and the throttle valve positioned to meter the correct quantity of fuel to the engine. The fuel control unit also meters fuel to the engine to control RPM, prevent overheating and surging, and prevent either rich blowout or lean dieout. Fuel delivery is automatically compensated for variation in altitude.

CHAPTER THREE

An air turbine driven starter geared to the N2 compressor is utilized for all engine ground starts. Air source to drive the starter can be either high pressure air (engines no.2 or no.3) or relatively low pressure air for any engine. The no.3 engine can be started from a high pressure air bottle in the right hand wheel well fairing or from an external source through a connection in the right hand wheel well aft fairing. There is a high pressure air bottle to start the no.2 engine in the left hand wheel well fairing.

Engine controls accessible to both pilots are in the control cabin. The engine start control switches and the ground start selector are on the overhead panel. The alternate low pressure start switches are on the flight engineer's lower panel, and the engine start levers on the pilots' control stand.

Turbofan thrust reversing is accomplished by a forward and aft thrust reverser. Each engine thrust lever has an additional handle which is used to actuate the two thrust reverser sections. When reverse thrust is required the engine thrust lever is retarded to the IDLE position and the reverse thrust lever pulled up and back. Further aft movement of the lever increases reverse thrust.

The pneumatic system provides high temperature compressed air conditioning and pressurizing of the aircraft and for low pressure engine starts. The system consists of turbocompressors mounted on engines no.2, 3 and 4 and low pressure bleed air from all four engines. The main air supply is obtained by compressing fresh air in the turbocompressors, which enters through ram inlets on the top of the engine nacelles. The turbocompressors are driven by bleed air from the last stage of the N2 high pressure compressor. The alternative air supply is obtained by bleeding low pressure air from the N1 intermediate compressor case of each engine. The compressed and heated air from each turbocompressor is routed through the pneumatic ducts to the air conditioning system.

The hydraulic power system supplies hydraulic fluid under pressure of 3000 psi to the hydraulically operated systems. Two separate and independent systems are used. They are designated as utility and auxiliary hydraulic systems.

The utility system supplies hydraulic power to the outboard spoilers, nose wheel steering, main wheel brakes, flaps, landing gear, and main gear levelling cylinder and snubber units. The auxiliary system supplies hydraulic power to the inboard spoilers, rudder power control system, and the main wheel brakes when the brake interconnect valve is open. A DC motor operated pump supplies hydraulic power to the main cargo door and to the brake system for ground handling operations.

The aircraft electrical power system consists of the AC power system, the DC power system, and generator constant speed drive system. Primary electrical power is supplied by the AC generators or alternators which are engine driven through constant speed drives. An external source may be used to supply AC requirements for ground operation. DC power is derived from the AC power system through transformer rectifier units. A battery supplies DC power for certain essential and control functions. Generator constant speed drives are independent hydraulic mechanical systems which convert the variable engine speeds to constant speed to obtain constant generator output frequency. The operation and monitoring of the electrical power system is accomplished by controls and indicators on the flight engineer's upper panel.

The main landing gear legs are hinged to trunnions mounted on the inboard face of a torque box which is cantilevered aft from the wing rear spar. This torque box is held between forged fore and aft members known as beaver tails. These lie along the top and bottom exterior surfaces of the wing, extending forward to about mid chord, and are bolted to the strengthened rib chords through the wing skins.

The CC137 aircraft has a tricycle landing gear system consisting of a dual wheel nose landing gear, and two main landing gear units, each consisting of a double axle truck with two pairs of wheels. The nose landing gear supports the forward end of the fuselage and provides directional control while the airplane is on the ground. The main landing gear, in conjunction with the nose landing gear, supports the airplane during ground operation. Moving the landing gear control handle to either the up or down position directs hydraulic pressure for landing gear actuation. When up is selected, the nose and main wheel well doors open, down locks release and the gear retracts. Up locks engage, and the wheel well doors close. To extend the landing gear, down is selected, the nose and main gear wheel well doors open, the gear extends and the doors close.

The nose gear is a steerable dual wheel assembly consisting of a shock strut assembly, drag brace, wheel

Boeing CC137 (707-347C)

Front view of nose landing gear and shock strut clamshell doors. Note that the main wheel well doors are closed.
(A. Stachiw)

Side view of nose landing gear. Note that the shock strut clamshell doors are open.
(A. Stachiw)

CHAPTER THREE

and tire assembly, a nose wheel snubber, nose gear actuator, lock mechanism, and a shock strut door and fairing assembly. It is hydraulically actuated to retract forward and up into the wheel well recessed into the lower nose compartment and is retracted or extended simultaneously with the main gear. The shock strut assembly absorbs the loads introduced into the nose gear while the aircraft is landing or taxiing, while the drag brace holds the nose gear in the up or down locked position.

The nose wheel steering system is the primary means of directional control during ground manoeuvring, effected by a steering wheel located on the side wall structure next to the pilot. The nose wheels may be turned approximately 60 degrees to either side powered by the landing gear hydraulic system. The nose wheels are turned straight ahead by cams as the oleo extends on takeoff, and hydraulic pressure to the steering system is cut off when the nose gear is not down and locked. The wheels may be released from the steering system by a quick disconnect.

The nose gear is raised and lowered by a hydraulic piston actuator. The cylinder end of the actuator is attached to a support shaft in the upper end of the nose wheel well, while the piston rod end is attached to a fitting on the upper aft side of the shock strut outer cylinder. The actuator extends to retract the gear and retracts to extend the gear. A lock mechanism is provided to lock the gear in either the gear up or gear down position, and to unlock the gear before retraction or extension. A snubber stops each wheel from continuing to rotate when the gear is retracted.

The wheels are forged aluminum and manufactured in separate halves to facilitate mounting the tubeless tires. The halves are bolted together and an O-ring seal is installed in a groove located radially out from the bolts to prevent air leakage. The wheels are mounted on a tapered axle with inner and outer roller bearing assemblies. They are equipped with 39 x 13 inch Type VII tubeless tires with 16 ply rating.

After retraction of the nose gear, the large wheel well is enclosed by clamshell doors. The shock strut area is covered by smaller clamshell doors. These are attached to the structure by two hinges on each door. The wheel well doors open only to allow the gear to retract or extend and are sequenced to close when the nose gear is up and locked or down and locked. The shock strut doors stay open when the gear is down and locked.

The main landing gear, in conjunction with the nose landing gear, supports the airplane during ground

Front view of main landing gear, port side. *(A. Stachiw)*

Side view of main landing gear, port side. *(A. Stachiw)*

Three-quarter rear view of main landing gear, port side. *(A. Stachiw)*

CHAPTER THREE

operation. Each main gear retracts inboard into the wheel wells in the fuselage, and is actuated by hydraulic power. Four wheels on each main gear truck carry the load of the aircraft with a minimum wheel size, and economize on the space required for retraction. The extension and retraction of the gear is controlled by a landing gear control handle located on the pilot's engine instrument panel. The guide has three positions, either up, down, or off.

The main gear trunnions transmit landing gear loads to the airplane structure and act as the hinge for retraction. The trunnions, pivoting on an axis parallel to the airplane centreline, provide the main attachment for the landing gear units. The shock strut cushions impact on landing, dampens vibrations and absorbs shock when the aircraft is taxiing or being towed.

The main gear wheel truck is a T-shaped tubular steel beam to which the forward and aft axles are attached. A jacking pad and a towing eye are formed on the forward and aft ends of the truck beam. The forward horizontal arms of the truck beam carry the two piece forward axle. The one piece aft axle is installed through the aft end of the truck beam and locked in position by two retaining plates. One large bolt attaches the truck to the shock strut.

The main gear wheels are forged aluminum split wheel assemblies for ease in mounting the tires. An air valve is sealed in the outer wheel half to permit inflation of the tires. The inner and outer wheel halves are bolted together with index marks in line and the joint sealed with a rubber packing. The wheel rotates on tapered wheel bearings. A felt seal is installed outside the bearing nearest the axle flange, while the outer bearing is sealed with a rubber seal and dust cap. The main gear tires are 46 x 16 inch, 28 ply rating Type VII tubeless tires.

The main gear truck leveling cylinder and snubber unit serve to return a tilted wheel to the perpendicular with the shock strut after a tilting force is removed. This assures landing gear alignment for retraction, and dampens pitching movement. The snubber acts to prevent rapid truck pitching movements.

The drag strut is a fixed length strut which gives fore and aft support to the shock strut. It is attached at the upper end to the trunnion by a special shear bolt designed to shear at excessive loads to prevent damage to the wing spars and fuel cells. Two clamps attached to the drag strut help support the shock strut doors. The torsion links prevent rotation between inner and outer shock strut cylinders which lock the gear truck parallel to the airplane centreline without affecting shock strut action. Action of the torsion links operates a safety switch for the electrical circuits of the brake antiskid system and the gear control handle lock system.

The side strut gives lateral support to the shock strut and is hinged to fold for retraction. It is attached at the upper end by a universal fitting to the floor beams in the wheel well. The upper attachment bolt also connects to the piston end of a side strut actuator. A cam secured to the upper attachment universal fitting also provides a connection to the emergency extension roller which pushes the gear to the down and locked position when emergency extension is used. The lower aft side of the side strut upper segment carries the gear downlock roller. The roller locks in a hook assembly when the gear is fully extended. Holes near the centre hinge of the upper and lower side strut segments accommodate a special ground downlock which prevents the side strut from unlocking and causing inadvertent gear retraction. The lower segment is attached by a universal fitting to the shock strut outer cylinder and is covered with a fairing to eliminate air noise in flight with the gear down.

The shock strut doors fair over the opening in the wing for the retraction paths of the shock and drag struts. The assembly consists of four doors attached to the shock and drag struts, which are actuated by direct attachment or linkage to main gear doors or structure. These doors are closed only on gear retraction.

The main gear actuator walking beam works in conjunction with the main gear actuator to retract and extend the main gear assembly. It serves to reduce the reaction force from the main gear actuator by taking it back to the trunnion through the walking beam. The gear actuator is a hydraulic piston with snubbing action to slow its movement when limits of travel are approached. The walking beam and actuator are located in the wing trailing edge just inboard of the trunnion and forward of the side strut. When the actuator is pressurized to extend, forces acting on the two trunnion arms rotate the trunnion counterclockwise (viewed from the aft) to swing the main gear inward and up into the wheel well. When the actuator is retracted the forces rotate the trunnion in the opposite direction to extend the gear.

The main gear side strut actuator extends to push the side strut overcentre into the locked position as the

Boeing CC137 (707-347C)

gear fully extends. On initial retraction the actuator pulls the side strut back from overcentre and out of the locked position. The actuator is a hydraulic piston and is located between the side strut upper universal and the wheel well structure.

After the gear control handle has been moved to the up or down position the main landing gear doors open. Movement of the doors positions the sequence valve to direct hydraulic pressure to the landing gear actuator components. Lines to the main and side strut actuators receive pressure simultaneously. Synchronized movement of the two actuators is obtained by providing a restrictor in the side strut actuator retraction line, and the side strut actuator starts to fold the side strut as the main gear begins to retract. A relief valve bypassing the restrictor permits rapid fluid flow from the side strut actuator to achieve free fall extension of the landing gear.

The main gear lock mechanism locks the main gear in the retracted or extended position. This is achieved by arrangement of a hook assembly to engage lock rollers on the main gear. An up lock roller is attached to the shock strut and a down lock roller to the side strut. A lock mechanism bungee exerts force on the lock roller to keep the hook assembly engaged, and to unlock the bungee, the lock actuator must overcome the pressure on the bungee. The lock actuator unlocks the gear to permit retraction or extension of the gear, and assures that the down lock roller remains engaged for ground operation.

The main gear wheel well doors fair over the fuselage wheel well opening when the landing gear is locked either up or down, and are operated by a hydraulic piston actuator. The main gear doors consist of two units, an inboard and an outboard half, hinged together by three hinges, with the inboard half being attached to the lower edge of the keel beam by four hinges. The doors are operated by the door actuator beam.

The aircraft is equipped with a hydraulic braking system. The brakes are multiple disc type, one being installed on each of the eight main wheels, and have automatic adjustment for lining wear. An anti-skid system prevents locked or skidding wheels when the brakes are applied on a landing surface. The brakes are actuated by applying pressure to the pilot's or copilot's rudder pedals. Corresponding pedals are interconnected by linkage under the cabin floor. Operating the right pedal(s) actuates the right brakes, and vice versa with the left pedal(s), and if either pair or all pedals are depressed, all brakes are applied simultaneously.

The brakes are used to slow the aircraft during its landing run, and automatic brake actuation is provided to stop the spinning wheels after the main gear is retracted on takeoff. The brakes also assist in turning the aircraft during ground manoeuvres. For parking, or during engine runup, a parking brake handle on the pilot's control stand holds the brakes on when the rudder pedals are released.

The hydraulic brake accumulator stores energy for brake operation, dampens pressure fluctuations, and provides instantaneous flow of fluid to the brake mechanism. When fully charged, the accumulator holds a reserve of fluid sufficient for five full brake applications. The accumulator is precharged with compressed air and uses fluid from either the utility or auxiliary hydraulic systems.

A pneumatic brake system is the alternate method of applying the main gear wheel brakes. This system bypasses the normal hydraulic brake system and has no antiskid control or directional control braking. It is operated by a handle on the captain's instrument panel which regulates the pressure for braking.

The primary flight controls on the CC137 aircraft are the ailerons, elevators, and rudder. These surfaces control the aircraft about its lateral, longitudinal and vertical axes, and are augmented by spoilers on the wings, wing flaps, and the adjustable horizontal stabilizer.

The control columns, both of which are cable interconnected for simultaneous movement, are used for primary flight control of the airplane about the longitudinal and lateral axes. Fore and aft movement of the column activates the elevators, while rotational movement of the control wheel actuates the ailerons and spoilers. Stops limit control column and control wheel movement. Stabilizer trim control, microphone and autopilot disengage switches are located on the control wheel.

The aileron control system provides lateral control about the airplane roll axis by operating two ailerons in each wing and controlling spoiler system operation. During low speed flight with extended flaps all lateral control surfaces are in operation. In high speed flight attitude flaps are retracted and outboard ailerons are locked out of the system. All ailerons are aerodynamically balanced against external surface air loads to minimize control forces required for system operation, requiring no hydraulic boost or electric servos. The inboard

CHAPTER THREE

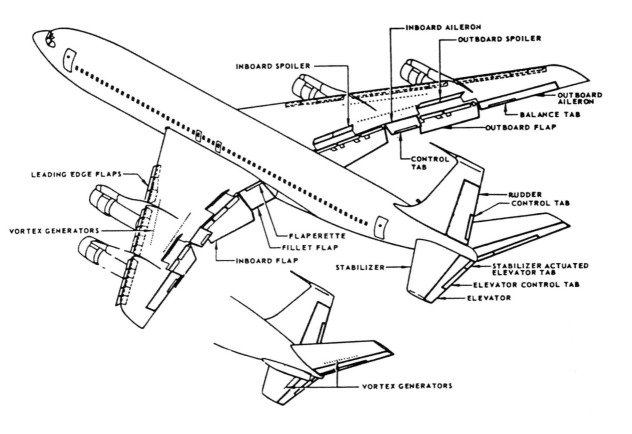

Primary flight controls, spoilers, and various high lift devices used on the Boeing CC137 aircraft. *(DND)*

ailerons are located between the inboard and outboard flaps at the trailing edge of the wing.

The outboard ailerons, in conjunction with the inboard ailerons and spoiler system provide lateral control during low speed flight, and are located in the trailing edge of the outer wing sections. Balance tabs reduce the force required to position and hold the outboard ailerons and are located in a cutout on the trailing edge.

The spoilers operate with the ailerons to provide lateral control about the roll axis of the aircraft. Four spoilers are located in the upper surface of each wing, in pairs forward of each of the main flaps. They are positioned hydraulically and are controlled by the aileron control system. The spoilers also act as speed brakes actuated by a control lever on the control stand. When used as speed brakes all are actuated simultaneously to created aerodynamic drag.

The elevator control system provides primary control of the airplane about its lateral axis. The elevators are positioned by means of control tabs without electrical or hydraulic power boosting, and are balanced to allow aerodynamic forces to assist in elevator movement during high speed flight. The system does allow for direct movement of the elevators during certain flight conditions and for ground operation without the aid of control tabs or balanced panels. Fore and aft movement of the control columns, which are interconnected, positions the control tabs, while aerodynamic forces on the control tabs and balance panels result in elevator displacement. A centering spring in the elevator control tab actuating mechanism provides artificial feel of elevator action. Each elevator functions independently of the other through its individual tab and linkage arrangement.

Boeing CC137 (707-347C)

The elevator control tabs convey aerodynamic forces to move the elevators and are located in the trailing edge of the elevator. They are statically balanced about the tab hinge centre line by means of nose weights which extend forward into the trailing edge of the elevators. The elevator balance panels are attached to each elevator nose by continuous hinges and project forward into bays in the horizontal stabilizers.

The horizontal stabilizer trim system controls the longitudinal trim of the aircraft by varying the incidence of the stabilizer. The stabilizer can be positioned by normal electrical or manual emergency control. A trim brake is used to arrest stabilizer out of trim motion when elevator control column movement opposes stabilizer trim movement. Normal control and operation of the stabilizer trim is accomplished with electrical power, while alternate control is accomplished by manual rotation of the stabilizer trim wheel.

The rudder, rudder control tab and rudder control system provide directional control to the aircraft. Rudder positioning is accomplished by a combination of hydraulic and mechanical systems. Under normal conditions the rudder is hydraulically positioned through full travel to either side. Feel is artificially supplied in the Power On condition. In the event of hydraulic failure, aerodynamic forces acting on the tab and rudder balance panels provide the force for positioning the rudder. The pilot feels aerodynamic tab hinge moments and system friction only.

The rudder control system is operated by two pairs of pedals which can be adjusted for pilot's comfort. Rudder pedal movement is transmitted to forward quadrants and jackshafts by pushrods. The forward quadrants are interconnected by a bus rod. Cables in turn transmit motion of the forward quadrant to the aft control quadrant located in the vertical stabilizer. Rotation of the aft control quadrant is transmitted by the rudder control linkage assembly to the power control unit actuating valve. The movement of the actuating valve causes the power control unit to operate and move the rudder.

The rudder impresses yawing moment on the aircraft. It is statically and dynamically balanced about the centreline of the rudder hinge by two balance weights and three balance panels located forward of the hinge point. These extend forward into the vertical stabilizer. The rudder control tab is used to control and trim the rudder. It controls air pressure distribution on the rudder surface causing the rudder to deflect. It is attached to the trailing edge spar of the rudder by hinges, and is statically balanced about its hinge centreline. The three balance panels assist rudder movement. They are located in the lower balance chambers of the vertical stabilizer.

The wing flap system provides high lift and low drag on takeoff and maximum lift and high drag on approach and let down. This is accomplished with moveable control surfaces on both leading and trailing edges of both wings.

View of Boeing CC137 on approach showing the wing flight controls and high lift devices to advantage.
(Canadian Forces)

CHAPTER THREE

Leading edge control surfaces consist of ten leading edge slats and three leading edge flaps located on the forward lower surface of each wing. They prevent high negative pressure rise on the forward upper surface of the wing at high angles of attack by shaping the airfoil to fit the airflow pattern. Both leading edge slats and flaps are hydraulically actuated and are controlled from a single control valve. The valve is controlled by the inboard and fillet flap drive system. This arrangement permits symmetrical operation of wing flaps when operated either by hydraulic or electrical power and prevents lateral unbalance. A warning horn system is provided to prevent takeoff with improperly positioned wing flaps, and is actuated when the flaps are positioned in other than the 10 to 20 degree range.

The trailing edge flap system consists of inboard and outboard double slotted main wing flaps and a single slotted fillet flap in each wing actuated by flap transmission assemblies. The transmission assemblies are driven by hydraulic motors through gear boxes and torque tubes. The inboard main flaps and fillet flaps, interconnected by torque tubes and gear boxes, are driven by a hydraulic motor. The outboard main flaps are interconnected and driven by a second hydraulic motor. Each hydraulic motor drives a power unit to operate the torque tubes and is individually controlled by a flap control valve connected to a common cable system, to a flap control lever on the cockpit control stand. Mechanical feedback of the flap position is incorporated into the control valve mechanism so flap operation is proportional to flap control lever movement and position. Lift characteristics of the trailing edge and fillet flaps are improved by cove lip doors on the underside of the wing trailing edge. These doors operate in unison with the flaps to maximum efficiency in laminar air flow throughout the operating range of the flaps.

The CC137 was equipped with a complete avionics suite.

COMMUNICATIONS SYSTEMS:
 HF and SELCAL, VHF, and UHF, Audio Intercom, and Audio PA systems.
RADAR SYSTEMS:
 Weather, Mapping and Search Radar, Radar Altimeter, Air Traffic Control Radar Beacon, and Radar Identification systems
NAVIGATION AIDS:
 Radio Compass, VOR / ILS, Marker Beacon,
 Homing Locator (Tanker), TACAN, LORAN, OMEGA
SEARCH AND RESCUE SYSTEMS:
 Underwater Beacon, and Emergency Beacon.

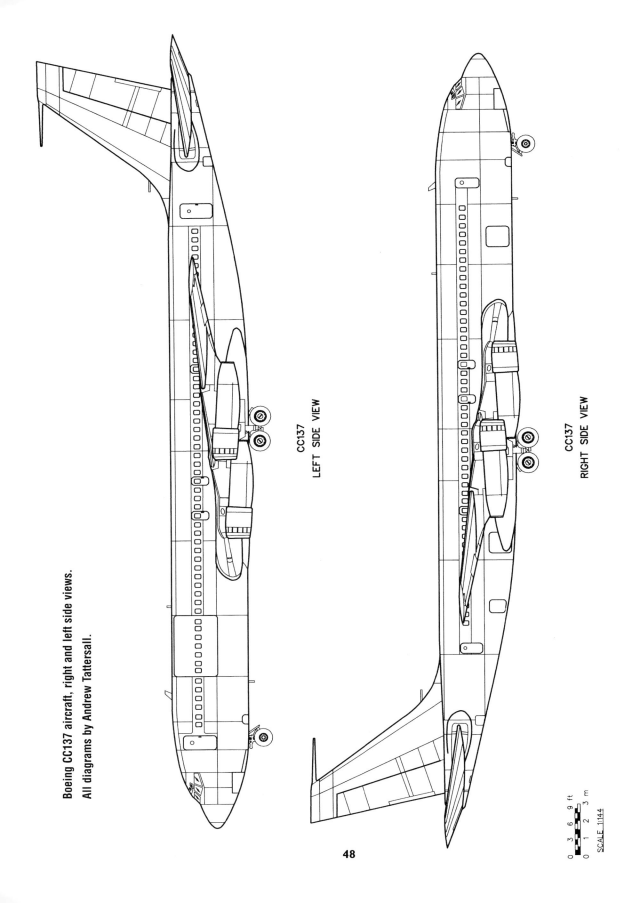

Boeing CC137 aircraft, right and left side views.
All diagrams by Andrew Tattersall.

CC137 LEFT SIDE VIEW

CC137 RIGHT SIDE VIEW

SCALE 1:144

Boeing CC137 front and NATO E-3A AWACS aircraft side view.

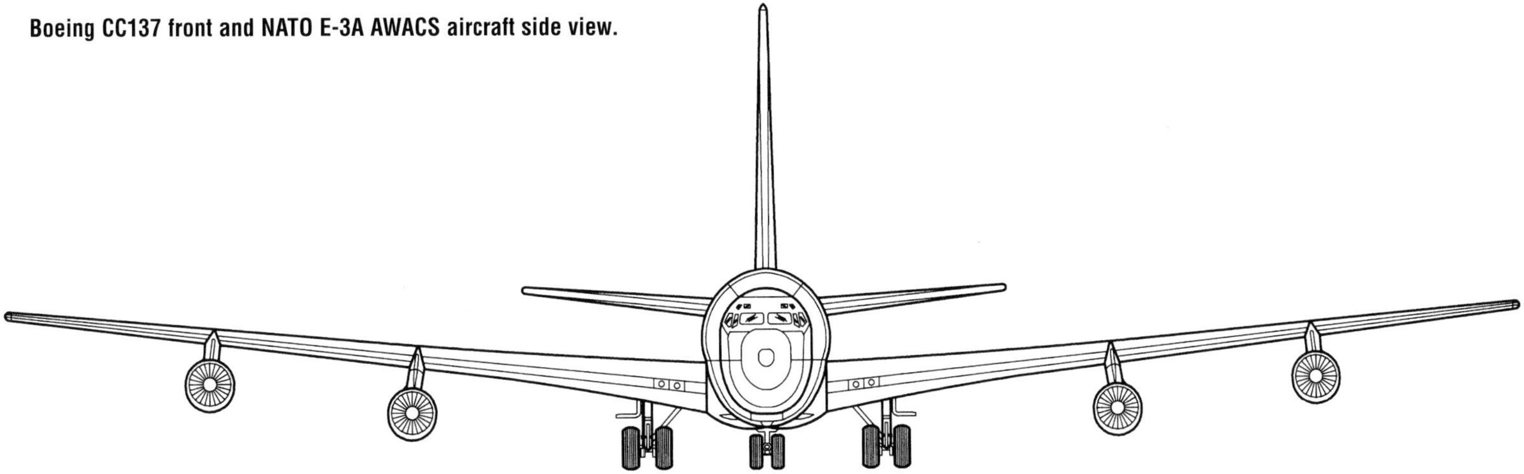

CC137
FRONT VIEW

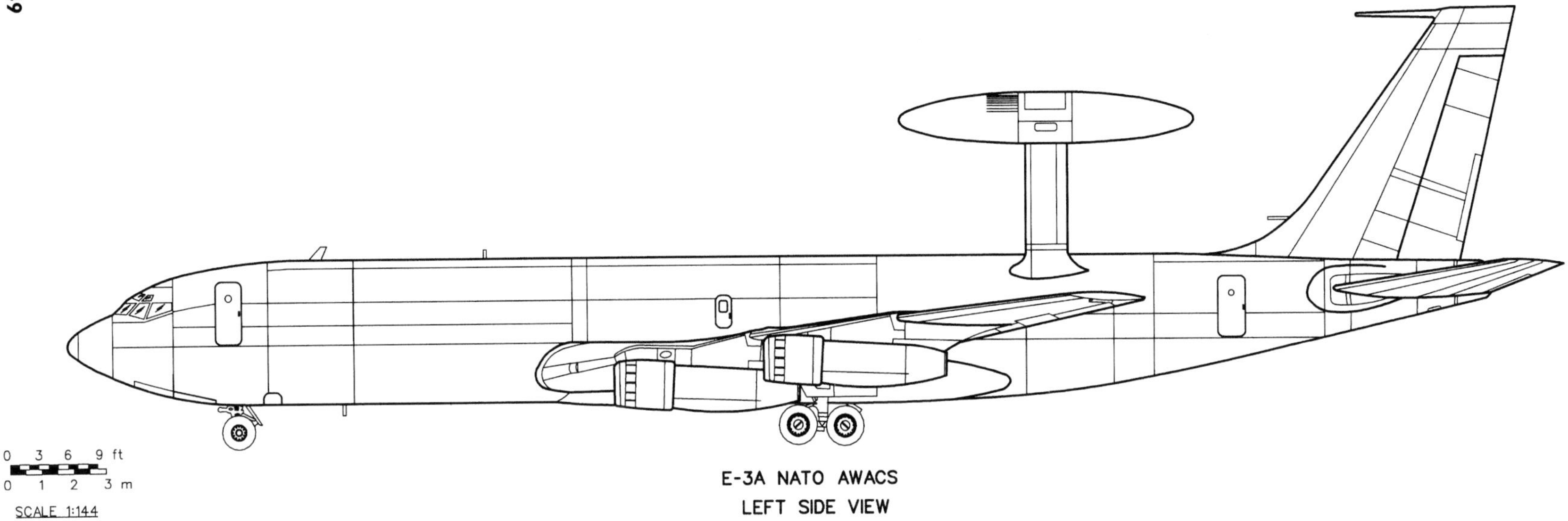

E-3A NATO AWACS
LEFT SIDE VIEW

SCALE 1:144

Boeing CC137 aircraft, top view.

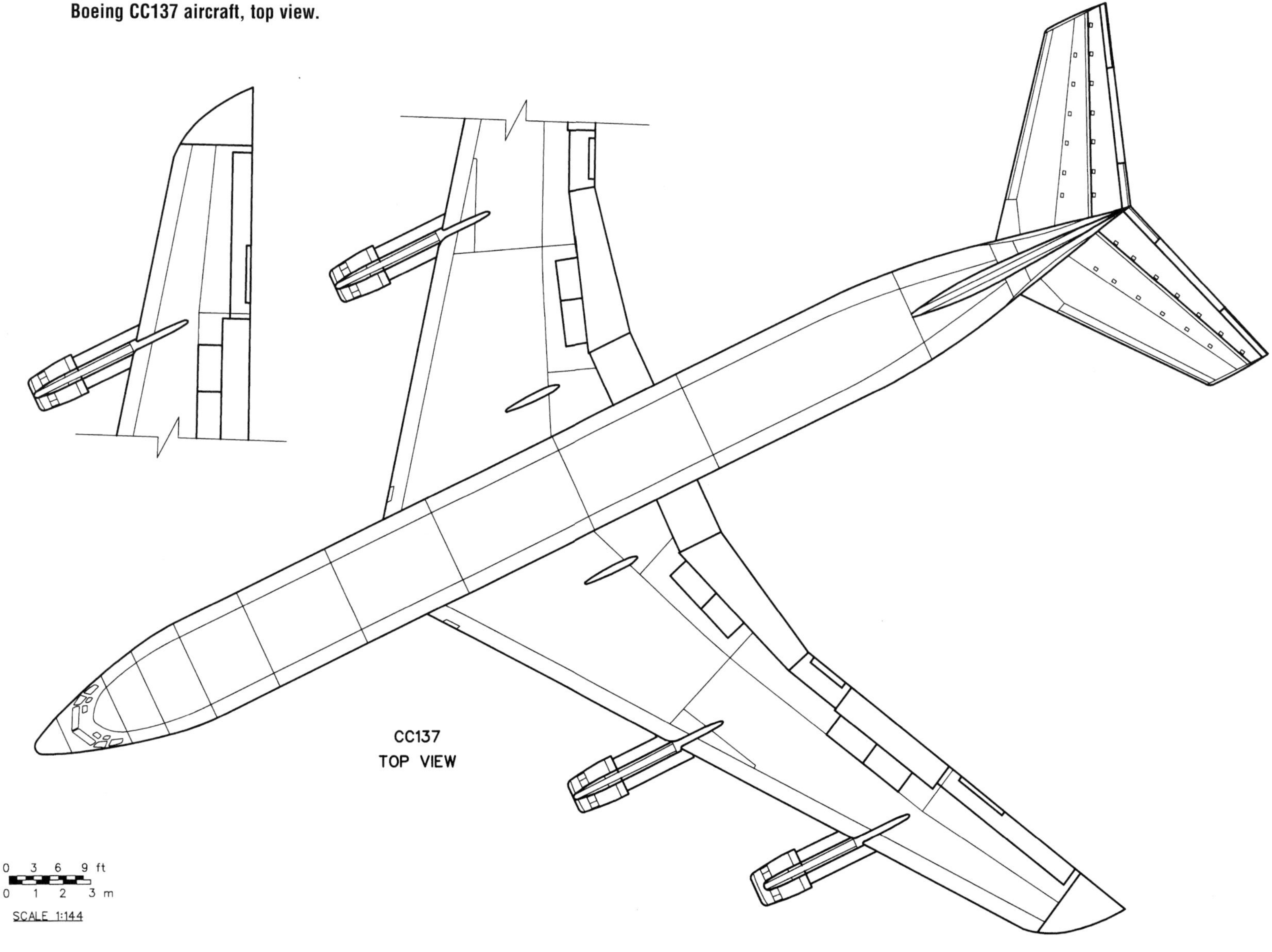

CC137
TOP VIEW

0 3 6 9 ft
0 1 2 3 m
SCALE 1:144

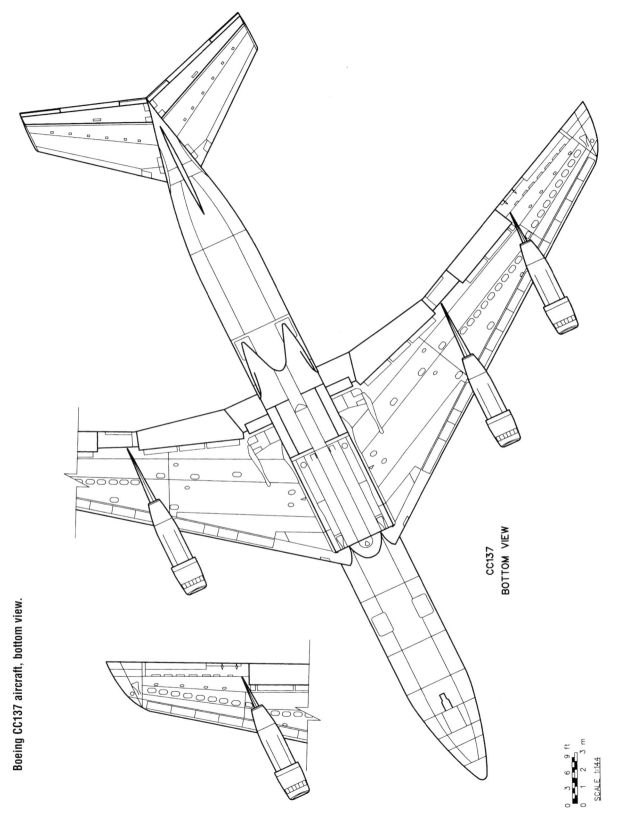

Boeing CC137 aircraft, bottom view.

CC137
BOTTOM VIEW

SCALE 1:144

Boeing CC137 aircraft, fuselage stations and sections, stabilizer and vertical fin diagrams

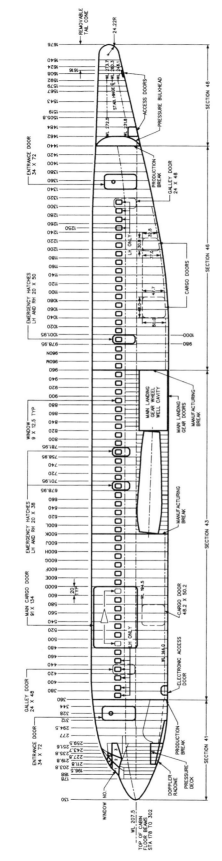
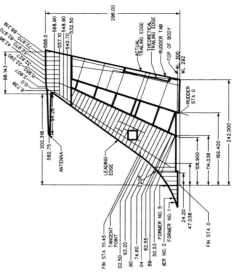
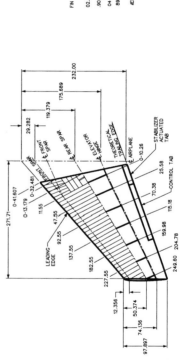

Boeing CC137 aircraft, wing diagram and sections.

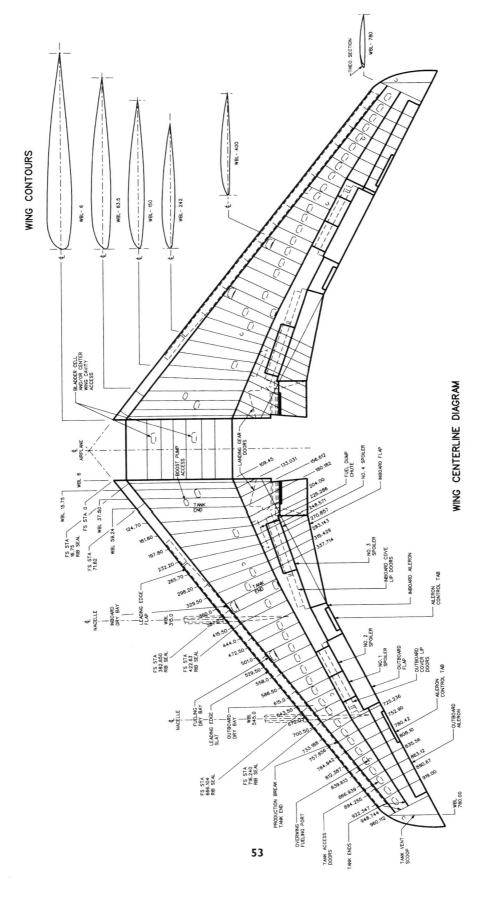

WING CONTOURS

WING CENTERLINE DIAGRAM

SCALE 1:144

CHAPTER FOUR

CC137 Squadrons and Units

Boeing CC137 13702 on takeoff on the occasion of its first flight from the Boeing facility at Renton, Washington. (DND)

448 TEST SQUADRON

Aeronautical Engineering Test Establishment (AETE)

As the flying unit of the Aeronautical Engineering Test Establishment (AETE), 448 Test Squadron was tasked with the technical evaluation of new aircraft for service with Canada's Armed Forces, test flying of new aircraft to establish flight parameters and procedures, and test flying of modifications incorporated in service aircraft. The unit was formed on 4 May 1967 at Cold Lake, Alberta, and incorporated in the Canadian Armed Forces on 1 February 1968. The squadron was disbanded on 1 September 1971, and all aircraft and personnel were absorbed by the Aeronautical Engineering Test Establishment. The Central Experimental and Proving Establishment (CEPE), as the higher establishment was previously named, had been based at RCAF Station Uplands before relocating to CFB Cold Lake.

When the contract was let to the Boeing Company for the CC137, AETE was tasked with the testing of the aircraft. With regard to the introduction of the CC137 into Canadian Forces service, time was of the essence, since the aircraft were near completion on the Boeing production line, and would be ready for acceptance tests within days.

CHAPTER FOUR

Within fifteen days, a crew had to be assembled, brought to the Boeing facility, and trained on the operation of the aircraft to begin the test flying program. Major Glen Personius, a USAF exchange officer on a two-year posting with AETE, had some 750 hrs. on the USAF KC-135 tanker aircraft, which was of the same aircraft family as the CC137. Since he was also an aeronautical engineer, he was chosen to head up the acceptance crew. The second pilot was Captain Walter Dennis, an Empire Test Pilot course graduate, whose experience had been largely on the CP107 Argus aircraft. The navigator for the first round of flights was Captain C.F. Johns, and for the second, Captain D.J. Anderson, an electrical engineering graduate of the University of Alberta. Flight Engineer was Warrant Officer Bob Neve.

Starting 10 February 1970, the crew began the process of evaluation by an intensive course of study and flying to enable them to test the aircraft. This consisted of 20 hrs. in the 707 simulator, 10 hrs. of flying the 707 aircraft, and lectures on the aircraft mechanical, electrical and hydraulic systems, as well as familiarization with the aircraft manuals. After the first round of test flights, a number of modifications were found to be necessary, resulting in a second set of flights. These modifications were mainly to meet Canadian Forces requirements in the repositioning of navigation equipment, which had not been called for by Western Airlines, the original customer for the aircraft. The work was completed by 7 April 1970, when the last of the first four aircraft was accepted.

Another view of Boeing CC137 13702 on climbout from the airfield during its first flight. *(DND)*

Boeing CC137 (707-347C)

Close-up of the 437(T) "Husky" Squadron badge aft of main passenger door on CC137 aircraft.

(LCol (ret'd) F. Chris Colton)

437 "Husky" Transport Squadron
426 "Thunderbird" Transport Training Squadron

Re-formed in the heavy transport role on 1 October 1961, 437 "Husky" Transport Squadron flew Canadair CC106 Yukon in the long range heavy transport and VIP transport roles. The squadron, based at RCAF Station Trenton on the north shore of Lake Ontario on the Bay of Quinte, was integrated into the Canadian Armed Forces on 1 February 1968. When the CC137 came into service with 437 Squadron in 1970, it supplemented, then replaced the CC106 Yukon, which was retired in April 1971.

All five aircraft were taken on strength by 437 Transport in the long range strategic transport role. The aircraft were flown on a regularly scheduled route between Air Movements Units in Canada, and to Gatwick in the U.K. and CFB Lahr in the Federal Republic of Germany. One flight continued on to Egypt to support the Canadian United Nations Expeditionary Force Detachment in the Middle East. Twice a year, the Canadian Battalion on duty in Cyprus was rotated, and troop lifts were carried out as a part of various exercises. Heavy lift was also carried out on Operation Boxtop, the resupply of Northern bases. The freight was carried as far as the USAF base at Thule, Greenland, where it was then forwarded by Canadian Forces CC130 Hercules aircraft.

The other primary role assigned to the CC137 fleet was that of long range VIP transport. Over the years the squadron provided transport to the Canadian Prime Minister and Cabinet Ministers, the Royal Family on official visits, and foreign dignitaries and heads of state.

The addition of the air-to-air refueling capability added a whole new dimension to the squadron's operations. By June 1973 the two tanker/transports (serial numbers 13703, 13704) were operational. This enabled the deployment of CF-5 Freedom Fighters to Norway to fulfill the commitment of the Canadian Forces to the defence of the Northern Flank of NATO, and later, for the deployment and operation of the CF-188 Hornet fighters.

The responsibility to train the flight crews, flight engineers, and maintenance personnel for the CC137 aircraft, as well as all other transport types in the Canadian Forces inventory, rested with 426 "Thunderbird"

CHAPTER FOUR

Transport Training Squadron. As well, when required, the squadron provided additional personnel for operational duties. For training purposes, the squadron borrowed aircraft from the operational squadrons, having none on strength for training alone.

The CC137 served with 437(T) Squadron throughout its service life. With the CC137, the squadron established an unsurpassed operational record in Air Transport Group, showing the Canadian flag on its worldwide schedule of operations. The CC137 was supplemented, and finally, replaced by the CC150 Polaris (Airbus Industrie A-310) in 1997. The squadron continues to uphold its motto Omnia Passem, or "Anything, Anywhere."

Boeing CC137 13703 tanker transport on departure from CFB Trenton configured for an air-to-air refuelling mission.
(Richard J. De Launais)

CHAPTER FIVE

CC137 Colour Schemes and Markings

Boeing CC137 13704 in the original Air Transport Command scheme refuels a pair of CF-5A Freedom Fighters. Note the original white finish scheme on the refuelling stores. *(DND)*

CHAPTER FIVE

Over the approximately 27 years that the CC137 fleet was in service with the Canadian Forces, the aircraft wore the "traditional" Air Transport Command colour scheme, with the distinctive Flash, which was a recognizable feature on Royal Canadian Air Force, and later, Canadian Armed Forces aircraft. The national markings applied to the aircraft underwent several detail changes which are described in this chapter.

Drawings were prepared documenting the patterns, colours, lettering and national markings featured on the aircraft. These drawings are identified following the descriptions of the various schemes.

Mr. Patrick Martin has prepared the definitive work on this subject titled Canadian Armed Forces, Aircraft Finish & Markings, 1968-1997. The book covers the finish schemes and markings applied to all Canadian Forces aircraft and should be consulted for the exhaustive treatment of this subject, with not only text and photographs, but representations of the official Canadian Forces drawings as well. One section is devoted to the CC137 aircraft, covering all the schemes that are described in this section.

The marking features presented in the following illustration are referred to in the text describing the various colour schemes in this chapter. The markings are as follows:

1. Red Shadow lettering CANADIAN FORCES / FORCES ARMÉES CANADIENNES
2. Black lettering AIR TRANSPORT COMMAND
3. ROUNDEL IDENT and ROUNDEL
4. CAF
5. Red Shadow Lettering CANADA
6. Canada Wordmark
7. Canadian Forces Signature
8. Canadian Flag, Bordered and Canadian Flag, Joined
9. UN Flag
10. Flash Pointed and Flash

Common markings featured on Canadian Forces CC137 aircraft.

Boeing CC137 (707-347C)

Port side view of Boeing CC137 13702 over the Rocky Mountains during acceptance trials out of the Boeing facility at Renton, Washington. Note the English language identification CANADIAN ARMED FORCES, and the wording AIR TRANSPORT COMMAND applied under the cargo door.

(DND, Neg. No.ISC70-2350)

Starboard side view of Boeing CC137 13702 over Puget Sound off the coast of Washington on an early training flight. Note the French language identification FORCES ARMEES CANADIENNES, and the absence of a French language equivalent to AIR TRANSPORT COMMAND.

(DND)

CHAPTER FIVE

5.1: CC137 Air Transport Command Finish Scheme

This finish and marking scheme was featured on the entire CC137 fleet when delivered from the factory.

5.1A: CC137 Air Transport Command Finish Scheme with Original Bilingual English / French Markings

The Air Transport Command finish scheme featured the upper fuselage and vertical stabilizer, including the rudder, and the upper surface of the wings, in CGSB White 513-101. The lower fuselage and lower surfaces of the wing were finished in Aluminum 8000-902. Inboard from the wingtips, CGSB Red 509-101 "search markings" panels were applied to both upper and lower surfaces, excluding the ailerons, as well as to the complete horizontal stabilizer, upper and lower, excluding the elevators. The engine pylons and pods were unfinished, as were the leading edges of the wings and vertical and horizontal stabilizers. The wing tip Beech 1080 refueling stores on aircraft 13703 and 13704 were, originally, finished overall CGSB White 513-101, with non-standard red/white/black flashes. These were later refinished in overall CGSB Red 509-101 with non-standard red/white/black flash.

The 20-inch flash, which in different forms was a recognizable feature on Canadian military aircraft since first being introduced after the Second World War, was applied to both sides of the fuselage encompassing the passenger windows. A 72-inch roundel was applied on the fuselage nose, both sides, within the flash. The wording CANADIAN ARMED FORCES was featured above the flash on the port side of the fuselage, and the French equivalent, FORCES ARMEES CANADIENNES, on the starboard side in the same relative position, in 21-inch Red Shadow lettering. The wording TRANSPORT COMMAND was applied on the port side under the cargo door in 10-inch letters, but no equivalent in French on the starboard side. The Last Three Numbers of the Aircraft Serial Number were applied on the outside face of both nose landing gear doors, and on both sides of the forward fuselage above the forward tip of the flash, both in 10-inch numerals. Aft of the main passenger door, port side, the 437(T) Squadron "Husky" Squadron Badge was applied, and the Canadian Coat of Arms was applied on the inside face of that door.

Aft of the rearmost exit door, port side, the wording Boeing 707 was applied with the 437 Squadron "Husky" Squadron Badge above it. A 48-inch roundel was applied to the upper surfaces of both wings. On the underside of

View of main passenger door area on forward port side of CC137 aircraft showing Canadian Coat of Arms on inside face of door and 437 Squadron "Husky" badge aft of door.

(LCol (ret'd) F. Chris Colton)

Boeing CC137 (707-347C)

the starboard wing, facing forward, CAF was applied in 48-inch letters and the Last Three Numbers of the Aircraft Serial Number on the underside of the port wing, also facing forward in 48-inch numerals. The 66-inch Canadian Flag with aluminum border was placed on each side of the vertical stabilizer, and the full Aircraft Serial Number was applied, each side, under the flag in 10-inch numerals. When the mission required, a United Nations lag was applied on each side of the vertical stabilizer under the aircraft serial number. Unless otherwise specified, all lettering and numerals were in CGSB Black 512-101.

This finish scheme was documented on Canadian Forces Drawing C70F00193, "Finish Scheme and Identification Markings Boeing 707 CC137 ACFT."

Note that this original scheme was declared illegal by the International Civil Aviation Organization because the aircraft were identified differently on opposite sides. This ruling resulted in the application of the "Air Transport Command Finish Scheme with Symmetrical Markings" which is described next.

5.1B: CC137 Air Transport Command Finish Scheme with Symmetrical Markings

This variant of the Air Transport Command finish scheme featured the upper fuselage and vertical stabilizer, including the rudder, in CGSB White 513-101, later FS.595 White 17875. The upper surfaces of the wing, which had been CGSB White 513-101, were refinished in CGSB Grey 201-103, including flaps and slats, but excluding ailerons. The finish on the lower fuselage and lower surfaces of the wings was changed from Aluminum 8000-902 to CGSB Aluminum 515-101, later, to CGSB Grey 201-103. Walkways were added to the upper surface of the wing adjacent to the fuselage. Inboard from the wingtips, CGSB Red 509-101, later FS.595 Red 11105, "search markings" panels were applied to both upper and lower surfaces, excluding the ailerons, as well as to the complete horizontal stabilizer, upper and lower, excluding the elevators. The engine pylons and pods were unfinished, as were the leading edges of the wings and vertical and horizontal stabilizers. The wing tip Beech 1080 refueling stores on aircraft 13703 and 13704 were finished in overall CGSB Red 509-101 with non-standard red/white/black flashes.

The 20-inch flash was retained on both sides of the fuselage, but the 72-inch roundel on the forward fuselage within the flash was replaced by a 72-inch roundel ident in the same position. The wording CANADIAN ARMED FORCES and FORCES ARMEES CANADIENNES, was replaced on both sides of the fuselage above the flash by a 20-inch CANADA in Red Shadow lettering in the same relative position. The wording TRANSPORT COMMAND

Boeing CC137 13703, one of the two tanker aircraft, on the ramp at CFB Trenton.
(Richard J. De Launais)

CHAPTER FIVE

Boeing CC137 13705 cruising over Lake Ontario near home base at CFB Trenton. *(DND)*

was deleted. The Last Three Numbers of the Aircraft Serial Number were applied on the outside face of both nose landing gear doors in 10-inch numerals. A 48-inch roundel was applied to the upper surface of the port wing facing forward and centered between the engine nacelles, and on the lower surface of the starboard wing facing forward and centered between the engine nacelles. The Last Three Numbers of the Aircraft Serial Number were applied in 48-inch numerals to the upper surface of the starboard wing, and to the lower surface of the port wing in the same relative position, parallel to the wing leading edge. The 66-inch Canadian Flag with aluminum border, or with no border and the outside red areas joined by a thin red line at top and bottom was placed on each side of the vertical stabilizer, and the full Aircraft Serial Number was applied, each side, under the flag in 10-inch numerals. When the mission required, a United Nations flag was applied on each side of the vertical stabilizer under the aircraft serial number. Aft of the main passenger door, port side, the 437(T) Squadron "Husky" Squadron Badge was applied, and the Canadian Coat of Arms was applied on the inside face of that door. Aft of the rearmost exit door, port side, the wording Boeing 707 was applied, with the 437 Squadron "Husky" Squadron Badge above it. Unless otherwise specified, all lettering and numerals were in CGSB Black 512-101.

This finish scheme was documented on Canadian Forces Drawing No.C72F00319, "Finish Scheme and Identification Markings Boeing 707 CC137 ACFT."

Cancelled, replaced by Drawing No. 8240499, "Finish Scheme and Identification Markings CC137 Boeing 707 AC."

5.1C: CC137 Air Transport Command Finish Scheme with Federal Identity Program Markings

This variant of the Air Transport Command finish scheme featured the upper fuselage and vertical stabilizer, including the rudder finished in FS.595 White 17875. The lower fuselage was finished in FS.595 Light Grey 16440. Inboard from the wingtips, were FS.595 Red 11105 "search markings" panels which were applied to both upper and lower surfaces, excluding the ailerons, as well as to the horizontal stabilizer, upper and lower, excluding the elevators. The wing tip Beech 1080 refueling stores were finished overall FS.595 Red 11105. Wing walkways were FS.595 Grey 36231. The engine pylons and pods were unfinished, as were the leading edges of the wings and vertical and horizontal stabilizers.

The 20-inch flash, was retained on both sides of the fuselage, and 72-inch roundel on the forward fuselage within the flash was placed in the same position as on the original scheme. The 762mm Canada Wordmark replaced the CANADA in the same relative position. The 406mm Canadian Forces Signature was applied under the flash above the wing on each side of the fuselage centered on the Canada Wordmark. A 48-inch roundel was applied to the upper surface of the port wing facing forward and centered between the engine nacelles, and

Boeing CC137 (707-347C)

Boeing CC137 13701 at low altitude over the forested terrain north of its base at CFB Trenton. *(DND)*

Boeing CC137 13701 in formation with an Airbus Industrie CC150 Polaris over a picturesque cloudscape. The Polaris aircraft replaced the CC137 in service with 437 "Husky" Squadron. *(DND)*

CHAPTER FIVE

on the lower surface of the starboard wing facing forward and centered between the engine nacelles. The Last Three Numbers of the Aircraft Serial Number were applied in 48-inch numerals to the upper surface of the starboard wing, and to the lower surface of the port wing in the same relative position, parallel to the wing leading edge. The 66-inch Canadian flag with aluminum border was placed on each side of the vertical stabilizer, and the full Aircraft Serial Number was applied, each side, under the flag in 10-inch numerals. When the mission required, a United Nations flag was applied on each side of the vertical stabilizer under the aircraft serial number. Aft of the main passenger door, port side, the 437(T) Squadron "Husky" Squadron Badge was applied, and the Canadian Coat of Arms was applied on the inside face of that door. Aft of the rearmost exit door, port side, the wording Boeing 707 was applied, with the 437 Squadron "Husky" Squadron Badge above it. Unless otherwise specified, all lettering and numerals were in CGSB Black 512-101.

This finish and marking scheme was first applied to aircraft 13704. The overhaul of the aircraft and engineering work was done by Monarch Engineering at Luton, England, in July, 1986. The aircraft was refinished by Sprayavia Ltd. The application of the markings on the wings, the placement of the roundel and the Last Three Numbers of the Aircraft Serial Number, was incorrect and was subsequently redone.

This finish scheme was documented on Canadian Forces Drawing No. 8240499 "Finish Scheme and Identification Markings CC137 Boeing 707 AC."

5.1D: CC137 Retirement Finish and Marking Scheme

This finish scheme, as applied to aircraft 13703, featured the 437 "Husky" emblem covering both sides of the vertical stabilizer of the aircraft. In all other respects, the aircraft was finished in the Definitive Finish and Marking Scheme described previously.

This finish scheme, other than the basic aircraft finish, was not documented on a Canadian Forces Drawing, and was applied to the aircraft by the squadron personnel to mark the retirement of the last of the aircraft fleet.

5.2: CC137 Variegated Camouflage Finish and Marking Scheme

This finish scheme was never applied to an aircraft, existing as a drawing package only. The two tanker aircraft (serial numbers 13703, 13704) were to be finished in a variegated colour scheme with the upper surfaces CGSB Green 503-301 (close to FS.595 34084) and CGSB Dark Grey 501-302 (close to FS.595 36118), with the whole underside finished in CGSB Grey 101-327. This scheme was prepared in reaction to the crisis in Poland, when the Soviet Union threatened to invade that country in response to the civil unrest occurring there.

Starboard side view of CC137 aircraft 13703 in the retirement colour scheme with the Husky mascot emblem on the tail.

(Andrew Cline)

Boeing CC137 (707-347C)

Port side view of CC137 "Showbird" aircraft 13703 in the retirement colour scheme on the ramp at Memphis, Tennessee ready for its penultimate refuelling mission during Exercise Lynx Leap on 30 January 1997.
(Andrew Cline)

View of retirement decoration on port side of tailplane representing the service of the aircraft with 437(T) Squadron and 8 Wing Trenton. The "1970–1996," as applied in October 1996, represented the years that the aircraft was in service, and was changed in November to read "1970–1997" when the retirement date was extended to April 1997.
(DND Neg. No. TNC-96-904-4)

CHAPTER FIVE

View of retirement decoration on starboard side of tailplane after the date change.
(A. Stachiw)

In the drawing, a full colour 12-inch roundel ident was applied on both sides of the nose of the aircraft, and a 6-inch CANADA, on both sides of the fuselage above the windows in the same relative position as on the Air Transport Command Scheme with Symmetrical Markings. The full colour 12-inch Canadian flag was placed on each side of the vertical stabilizer, and the full Aircraft Serial Number was applied under the flag. A full colour 16-inch roundel was applied on the upper surface of both wings. On the underside of the starboard wing, CAF was applied in 16-inch letters facing forward, and on the underside of the port wing, the Last Three Numbers of the Aircraft Serial Number, in 16-inch numerals, also facing forward. All lettering and numerals were to be in CGSB Black 512-301.

This finish scheme was documented on Canadian Forces Drawing No. DDDS 1023 "Finish Scheme and Ident Markings, Camof (Variegated) CC137 AC."

5.3: CC137 Tactical Finish and Marking Scheme

This finish scheme was never applied to an aircraft, existing as a drawing package only. The aircraft was to be finished with a straight line definition between the upper surface colour semi-gloss Grey Tempo 4700-BB-63 (FS.595 25237) and the lower surface colour semi-gloss Grey Tempo 4800-B-111.

The markings were to be applied using the lower surface colour semi-gloss Grey Tempo 4800-B-111 on the upper surfaces, and the upper surface colour semi-gloss Grey Tempo 4700-BB-63 (FS.595 25237) on the lower surfaces. In the drawing, a 72-inch low viz roundel was applied on the fuselage nose, both sides, in the same position on the forward fuselage as on the definitive scheme. A 762mm Canada Wordmark was placed on each side of the fuselage above the windows over the wing and a 406mm Canadian Forces Signature was applied under the flash above the wing on each side of the fuselage centered on the Canada Wordmark. A 66-inch low viz Canadian flag, with the full Aircraft Serial Number in 10-inch numerals under the flag, was placed on each side of the vertical stabilizer. A 48-inch low viz roundel was applied to the upper surface of the port wing facing forward and centered between the engine nacelles, and on the lower surface of the starboard wing facing forward and centered between the engine nacelles. The Last Three Numbers of the Aircraft Serial Number were applied in 48-inch numerals to the upper surface of the starboard wing, and to the lower surface of the port wing in the same relative position, parallel to the wing leading edge.

This finish scheme was documented on Canadian Forces Drawing No. 8440233 "Finish Scheme and Ident Markings, Tactical, CC137 Boeing 707AC."

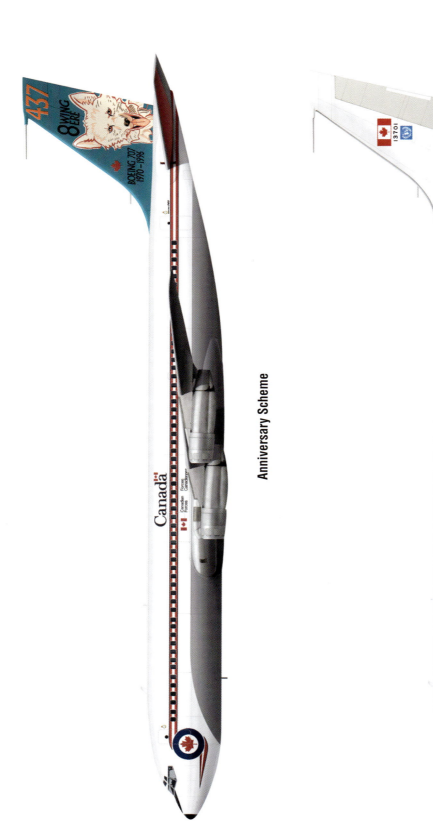

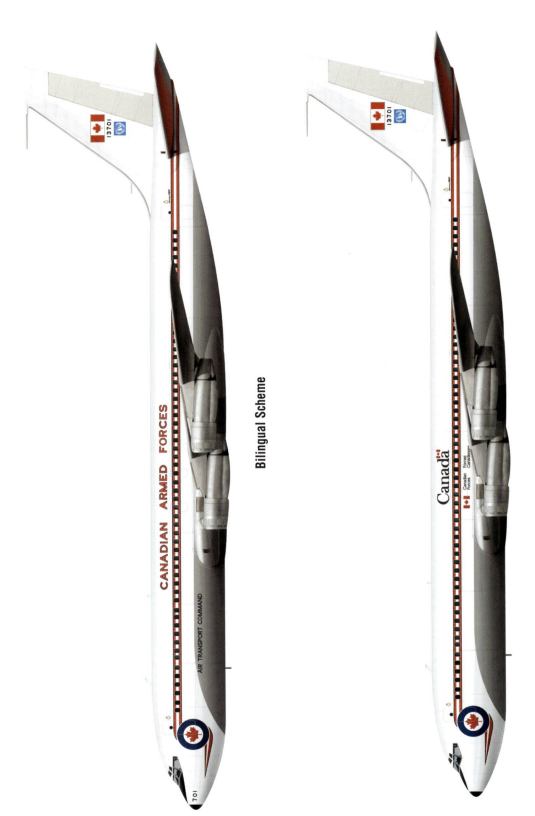

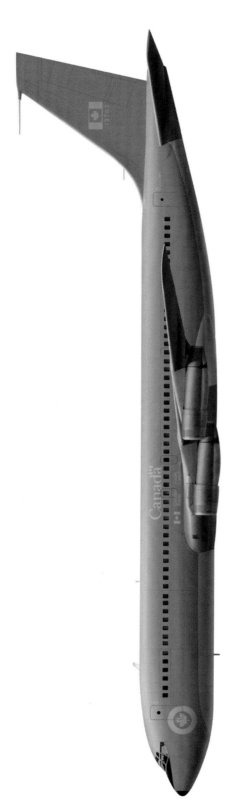

Tactical Scheme

Variegated Scheme

Illustrations by Stephen Otvos

CHAPTER SIX
Air-to-Air Refuelling System

View against a perfect sky of a CC137 tanker refuelling a CF-5A Freedom Fighter of 434 TAC(F) Squadron and a CF-18A from the Aeronautical Engineering and Test Establishment.
(DND Neg. No. REC-89-829)

Beech 1080 wingtip fueling store configuration.

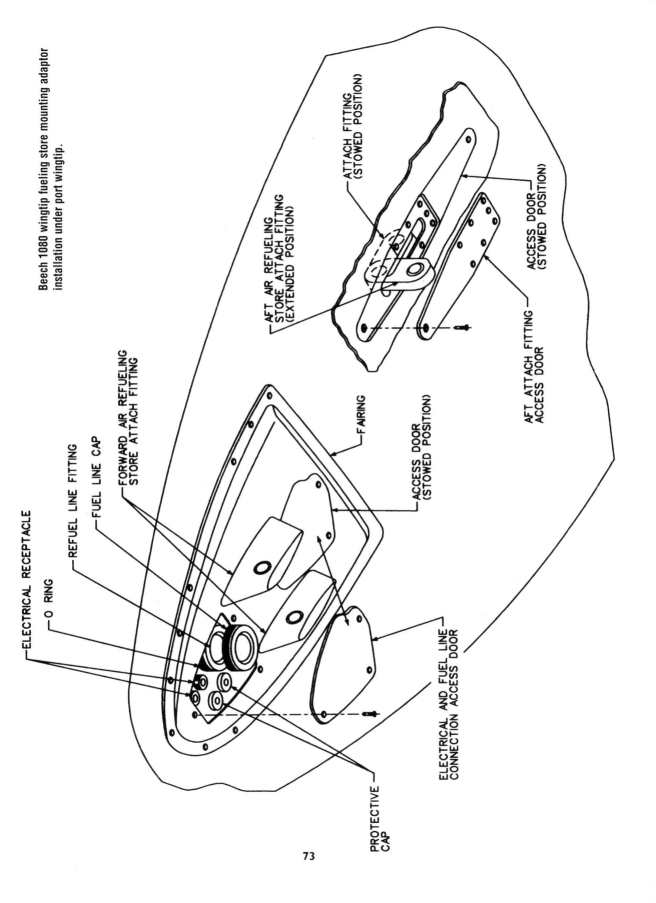

Beech 1080 wingtip fueling store mounting adaptor installation under port wingtip.

Boeing CC137 (707-347C)

In 1971, at the Boeing Aircraft Company plant, two CC137 aircraft, serial numbers 13703 and 13704, were equipped with an air-to-air refueling system featuring Beech Model 1080 refueling pods. The stores were removable, and when installed were attached to the fittings in the underside of each wing tip. The wing spars were extended to the wing tips to support the wingtip refueling pods installations, and the store stations located under each wing tip were modified to accept the refueling kit stores. This necessitated the relocation of the wingtip magnetic compass flux valves to the vertical stabilizer. The installation of the kits required additional plumbing as well as structural modifications. An air refuelling manifold was run from the centre wing tank through to the wing tip pod installation and hydraulic fuel pumps were installed which decreased the capacity of the centre fuel tank from 67,000 lbs. to 60,000 lbs. of fuel. Additional exterior lighting was installed to illuminate the vertical stabilizer, both upper and lower wing surfaces, the engine pods, and the refuelling pods.

Initially, because the pods were mounted at the tips of the highly flexible wing, they were susceptible to oscillation. This was amplified in the trailing basket as the receiving fighter sought to engage. Furthermore, the deployed drogue created a 25 percent increase in drag, and internal differences in the basket prevented the system from being used by other than CF aircraft. Most of these problems had been corrected by January 1973.

The installation of TACAN equipment in the CC137 tanker enabled the fighters to home in for the refuelling rendezvous, the tanker acting as a mobile TACAN installation in the sky. Two observer stations were added, one on each side aft of the passenger cabin. The engineer sat, facing aft, on the starboard side of the fuselage, and a navigator, responsible for the fighter flight, sat facing aft on the port side of the fuselage. Once it had homed onto the CC137 tanker aircraft, the fighter aircraft lined up behind the trailing basket, guided by indicator lights on the pod and advanced to the contact position. Once contact was made with the basket by the receiving fighter aircraft, the hose advanced and retracted automatically to compensate for deviations in position. A white band marked the centre of the hose length and white and orange stripes marked the inner and outer limits of extension.

View of underside of port wing tip showing adaptor for refuelling store installation.
(A. Stachiw)

CHAPTER SIX

Each store was 18 feet long and 25 inches in diameter. A boom was lowered from the underside of the pod extending 390 downward during the refueling operation and a drogue at the end of a hose was reeled out to an approximate distance of 35 ft. A light was installed at the end of the boom to assist the pilot of the probe-equipped receiving aircraft in engaging the drogue. In the nose of the pod was a four-bladed ram air turbine which drove the fuel pump.

The air refuelling system consisted of two separate subsystems to permit air-to-air refuelling of two receiver aircraft. One subsystem supplied fuel to the left wing air refuelling store and the other to the right wing refuelling store. Both systems supplied fuel from the centre wing tank, however additional fuel from main tanks No. 2 and No. 3 was transferrable to the centre wing tank.

The primary air refuelling controls were located on the flight engineer's auxiliary side panel. The lower panel had two fuel "quantity delivered" indicators in addition to the normal fuel quantity indicators and controls. Related hydraulic controls and indicators were located on the lower panel as well.

View, from front, of Beech 1080 wingtip refueling store under port wing. Note ram air turbine in the nose of the pod and boom in retracted position on the underside.

(A. Stachiw)

Boeing CC137 (707-347C)

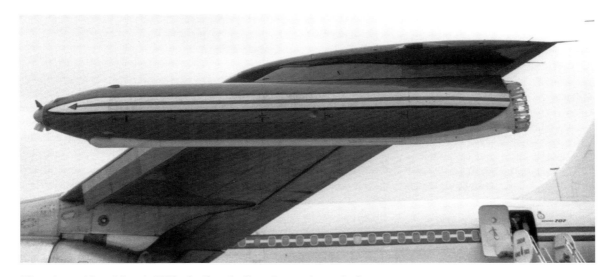

View, from side, of Beech 1080 wingtip refueling store under port wing. *(A. Stachiw)*

View, from rear, of Beech 1080 wingtip refueling store under port wing. Note the drogue in stowed position in the end of the pod.

(A. Stachiw)

CHAPTER SIX

Getting ready for air-to-air refuelling operations at CFB Trenton, 13703 has its Hose and Drogue Units (HDU) installed, June 20, 1996.

(Andrew Cline)

Boeing CC137 (707-347C)

Refuelling pod technicians MCpl. Lloyd Meier and Cpl. Chuck Rickard preflight the Hose and Drogue Units of 13703 on the ramp at Memphis.

(Andrew Cline)

"Catching the Basket." CF188 Hornet 188748 from CFB Bagotville pulls up to take on fuel from Boeing 13703 on 7 February 1996 over New York State.

(Andrew Cline)

CHAPTER SIX

On 30 January 1997 on Exercise Lynx Leap, two groups of CF188 Hornet aircraft from 416 Squadron were flown from Eglin AFB, Florida, to CFB Cold Lake, refuelling twice enroute. The first, at 20 minutes north of Memphis, and the second over the Dakotas, involved the transfer of 4000 pounds of fuel. CF188B 188937 is seen here being tanked up.
(Andrew Cline)

CHAPTER SEVEN

Canadian Forces and the NATO AWACS

NATO E-3A Sentry AWACS aircraft 90442, climbing out from CFB Trenton at the Astra Air Show in 1987. *(A. Stachiw)*

CHAPTER SEVEN

US Air Force Boeing E-3A Sentry of the 552nd AWACW, Tinker AFB, OK. This is the Commander's aircraft at CFB North Bay, ON, for familiarization flights for 22nd NORAD Region personnel, December 2, 1998. A large Canadian component serves on these aircraft from Tinker and Elmendorf AFB, AK. *(Andrew Cline)*

The NATO E-3 Sentry Airborne Warning and Control System (AWACS) was designed to strengthen and improve the air defence of Europe. This highly mobile and survivable surveillance system is based on a fleet of 18 E-3A Sentry AWACS aircraft as well as support equipment and trainers, including three Boeing 707 Trainer/Cargo aircraft.

Canada is one of 12 of the 19 NATO member nations that funds the NATO Airborne Early Warning Force E-3A component. The 12 are Belgium, Canada, Denmark, Germany, Greece, Italy, Luxembourg, the Netherlands, Norway, Portugal, Turkey, and the United States. There are 150 Canadian Forces personnel assigned to the program, the third largest group. The E-3D component, consisting of 6 aircraft, based at Waddington, represents the United Kingdom's contribution to the program. It is manned by RAF personnel only.

Each aircraft has a crew of 17, with four flight crew members;
2 Pilots
1 Navigator
1 Flight Engineer
and 13 mission crew members;
    1 Tactical director
    1 Fighter Allocator
    2 Weapons Controllers
    2 Surveillance Control Officers
    2 Surveillance Operators
    1 Communications Operator
    1 Communications Technician
    1 Radar Technician
    1 Computer Display Technician
    and one other.

This number may vary according to the specific mission.

NATO AWACS FLEET STATISTICS

USAF Serial Number	NATO Fleet Number	TOS
90442	N-1	82.2.24
90443	N-2	82.5.19
90444	N-3	82.8.19
90445	N-4	82.11.16
90446	N-5	82.3.11
90447	N-6	83.6.8
90448	N-7	83.7.6
90449	N-8	83.8.19
90450	N-9	83.10.25
90451	N-10	84.1.24
90452	N-11	84.5.3
90453	N-12	84.5.22
90454	N-13	84.11.2
90455	N-14	84.10.
90456	N-15	84.11.9
90457	N-16	85.2.
90458	N-17	85.4.
90459	N-18	85.6

And 3 707-320C Trainer Aircraft

Boeing CC137 (707-347C)

In the late 1960s it was recognized that the low altitude penetration capabilities of the Warsaw Pact air elements was a significant threat to the security of the countries in the NATO Alliance. The NATO organization defined a requirement to provide an improved early warning and detection system against this threat, which was not being adequately addressed by the existing fixed base or mobile early warning radars. The answer to the problem was to use an airborne early warning system that possessed radar with long range and look down capability, with the ability to detect and track moving targets amidst the ground clutter returns that degraded and confused existing air defence radars.

NATO studies carried out between 1971 and 1975 resulted in the choice of the U.S. Air Force E-3A from the competing Air Early Warning Systems as offering the most suitable operational solution. The multinational provisional Airborne Early Warning and Control (AEW&C) Program Office was established by the NATO defence ministers in 1975.

The NATO AWACS aircraft required modifications to suit the European environment. These modifications, combined with enhancements that had been planned for USAF E-3A aircraft, formed the basis of the standard AWACS configuration. The program featured a single development plan with both the U.S. Air Force and NATO adopting the same configuration. This met the objectives of interoperability and standardization of the two fleets.

In 1978, when development of the standard configuration E-3A was initiated, the various national governments performed an in-depth review of the proposal and arrived at an agreement on acquisition and cost sharing. At a meeting in December 1978, a multilateral memorandum of understanding was drafted to acquire a NATO owned Airborne Early Warning and Control System. The NATO AEW&C Program Management Organization was established to manage the program to acquire the fleet of 18 aircraft, support equipment and trainers. As well, the organization was assigned the responsibility to modify the existing NATO air defence ground environment system necessary to provide interoperability and data exchange. The NATO AEWF Command was formed in October 1980, with its headquarters co-located with SHAPE. In addition, the force comprises two operational components, the E-3A component at Geilenkirchen NATO Air Base in Germany

A NATO E-3A Sentry AWACS, 90448, with enhanced electronic capabilities. *(Bill Scobie)*

CHAPTER SEVEN

Boeing E-3B Sentry 76-1605 963-/964/965ACS, 552nd ACW, ACC, Tinker Air Force Base, OK. This is the Wing Commander's aircraft at the USAF 50th Anniversary Golden Air Tattoo, Nellis AFB, NV, April 24, 1997.
(Andrew Cline)

(as well as maintenance and repair facilities), and the E-3D component at RAF Waddington in the U.K. There are three Forward Operating Bases located in Greece, Italy and Turkey, and a Forward Operating Location in Norway. In addition, a training facility was constructed to assist the multinational force operating the NATO E-3A fleet.

The NATO AWACS was developed from the successful USAF E-3A Sentry. The aircraft is equipped with a sophisticated radar capable of detecting both high and low flying aircraft at ranges up to 400 kilometres (249 miles) when flying at an altitude of 9,000 metres (29,529 ft.). Its surveillance volume is scanned by the identification friend or foe (IFF) system to provide a means of distinguishing friendly from hostile aircraft. The antennas from both systems are housed in a rotating 9.1 metre rotating radome mounted above the fuselage, forward of the tailplane, that rotates every ten seconds, providing 360 degree coverage.

Sophisticated avionics equipment for navigation, communication, data processing and display are integrated into a Boeing 707-320B airframe which has been modified to accommodate the mission equipment and a crew of 17. The NATO aircraft are equipped with the same Pratt & Whitney TF33-PW-100A turbofan engines as those installed in the USAF aircraft.

All NATO and USAF aircraft delivered in and after December 1981 were in the standard configuration. This configuration features enhanced radar capable of detecting airborne targets in clutter and maritime

Boeing CC137 (707-347C)

vessels. The communication links were further improved by the addition of the JTIDS (Joint Tactical Information Distribution System) which allows a large volume of information to be transmitted in seconds to multiple clients. This system employs special technology to protect against electronic jamming and enemy eavesdropping. The AWACS computer was enhanced to increase its capacity and operating speed, allowing the operational computer programs to expand their functions and to provide increased target track handling and communications processing. The first NATO E-3 was delivered in January, 1982, and the final eighteenth aircraft on 25 April 1985, ahead of schedule and below the contract price.

In January 1993 Boeing was awarded a $294.6 million contract for the Mod Block 1 phase of the NATO E-3 modernization program. This involves three major enhancements to the system capabilities. These include colour displays to improve the form and usability of incoming situational information, and Have Quick radios add secure and anti-jam features to the UHF communication system. A version of the JTIDS, called Link 16 increases the amount of information that can be collected and shared between two AWACS aircraft. This refit was completed in November 1997.

NATO has also joined the Radar System Improvement Program, which will improve the E-3 radar by increasing the sensitivity of the pulse Doppler radar, enabling the detection of small stealthy targets over a longer range, and improving the ECM capability. Operational testing was completed in September 1996 and completed in the entire fleet in 1999.

In November 1997 Boeing was contracted to develop and test the next mission systems upgrade for the NATO fleet. Under the mid term engineering, manufacturing and development contract, major systems-related enhancements to computers, displays, communications, navigation and target identification will be integrated. Retrofit of the entire fleet will be implemented in a follow-on contract.

On 5 July 2001 the European Aeronautics and Space Company Military Aircraft signed an agreement with Northrop Grumman, Pratt & Whitney, and Seven Q Seven Inc., to pursue a Request for Information issued by the NATO executive agency NAPMA to re-engine the complete NATO E-3 fleet and three 707 trainer aircraft. The commercial off the shelf certified Pratt & Whitney JT8D-219 turbofan engines will replace the Pratt & Whitney JT-3D 7 and TF33 engines now installed.

The system will be certified on a Boeing 707-300 series aircraft, which is representative of the airframe for the E-3 AWACS fleet. This upgrade will not only enhance the performance and range capability of the fleet, but put into service the most widely used commercial engine currently in operation, which meets or exceeds all ICAO limits emissions and FAR Stage Four noise limits. This retrofit, along with the other systems upgrades, would ensure that the E-3 will continue to be an invaluable and viable surveillance asset well into the twenty-first century.

CHAPTER EIGHT
Long Range Patrol Aircraft

An artist's impression of the Long Range Patrol Aircraft in Canadian Forces Service with the traditional colour scheme that was in use on the CP107 Argus aircraft at that time.

(Boeing Airplane Company)

Boeing CC137 (707-347C)

The Canadair CP107 Argus Mk. 1. The Long Range Patrol Aircraft competition was initiated to replace the 32 aircraft Argus fleet.

(Canadair Ltd.)

In the early 1970s, the Canadian Forces began the process to select a replacement for the Canadair CP107 Argus long range patrol aircraft fleet. The cost of maintaining and operating the piston engined Argus had become prohibitive, as, for example, the 100/130 AVGAS used was becoming difficult to obtain. After the government rejected a study involvng the rebuilding of the Argus and retrofit with turbine powerplants, several aircraft companies submitted proposals. The Boeing Aircraft Company submission was named the 707-LRPA. Other contenders were Breguet (France) with the Brequet (Dassault) ATL.2 Atlantique; Hawker Siddeley (U.K.), with the HS.801 Nimrod; Lockheed Aircraft Corporation (USA), with the P-3 Orion; and McDonnell Douglas (USA), with a variant of the KC-10 Extender. The Boeing proposal was also aimed at a similar Australian requirement to replace its fleet of Lockheed P2H Neptune and Lockheed Orion P-3A and P-3B patrol aircraft.

In order to prove the concept, Boeing acquired a 720-025 model, c/n 18158, from a charter operator (Trans Polar LN-TUW) in the autumn of 1971. The aircraft, registered N3183B, was configured as a prototype for the defined LRPA, which would be based on the larger 707-320C variant. The 720 had a maximum gross weight of 230,000 lbs., versus 334,500 for the 707-320C. As well, the 707-320C was some 15 ft. longer, and had a 15 ft. longer wingspan.

The aircraft was equipped with Magnetic Anomaly Detection gear (MAD) installed in the wing tips, sonobuoy launching and storage facilities, tactical crew stations, and crew comfort accommodations. After a layup of some four months, during which these installations were fitted, the flight program began in April 1972. In the test program, the aircraft was flown at 200 ft. over water and performed 40 degree banks in simulated anti submarine warfare (ASW) manoeuvering. As well, sonobuoys were dropped from altitudes as high as 40,000 ft., at speeds of 400 kts. Allowing for reasonable requirement for dash to targets and reserves, the aircraft could remain on station for 8-10 hrs. at a distance of 1,000 nautical miles from base.

During the initial phase, the development of a dual channel autopilot based on the Sperry SPZ-1 used in the Boeing 747 was completed and ASW modes demonstrated. The automatic flight control system was introduced to reduce the pilot's workload and to increase safety in the long duration low altitude ASW missions. The tentative navigation system, incorporating Inertial Navigation System (INS), Omega, and Doppler was tested and proven in long range flights and simulated ASW exercises.

CHAPTER EIGHT

The pilot's tactical display was to be installed on the centre instrument panel to interface with the Inertial Navigation System, but also having the capability of being driven by a central tactical data processor.

The dual Magnetic Anomaly Detection (MAD) gear installation, incorporating 5 ft. booms in each wingtip, projected aft, was proven capable of locating a magnetic disturbance in one pass. Several sonobuoy launches were made from two launch tubes, one installed vertically, and the other at a 30 degree angle, with the same result. These were obtained using both cartridge activated devices from altitudes from 1,000 ft. to 40,000 ft. and airspeeds to 400 knots, as well as free fall drops from below 3,000 ft. at speeds from 180 to 240 knots.

The advanced ASW mission envisioned by company planners demanded greater payload than existing ASW aircraft, as well as longer range, more time on station, higher altitude capability, and greater dash speed. Furthermore, a multi-mission requirement, including strategic transport and air-to-air refuelling was taken into consideration.

The Canadian requirement was the biggest ever peacetime contract. Requests for proposals, issued in September 1972, required an aircraft with a broad range of capabilities, both military and civilian. When cutbacks in defence funding and a shift in defence policy were announced by Prime Minister Trudeau on 6 April 1969, and explained in detail in the government's White Paper on Defence published in August 1970, priority was given to the defence of North America and the maintenance of Canadian sovereignty. As a consequence, the requirement went beyond an ASW platform, taking the form of a multi-mission reconnaissance weapon system. The missions included, as well as ASW, detecting unwanted intrusions into the Arctic, detection of oil spillage and dumping, wildlife management and cataloguing, and ice reconnaissance.

For these tasks, Boeing identified a wide spectrum of sensors, radar, infrared sensors, and optical devices. Medium resolution side looking radar, which has an all weather capability, was included for the detection of manmade objects in the Arctic environment. The

Cutaway illustration of the Long Range Patrol Aircraft showing the basic interior arrangement.
(Boeing Airplane Company)

General arrangement of the Long Range Patrol Aircraft. *(Boeing Airplane Company)*

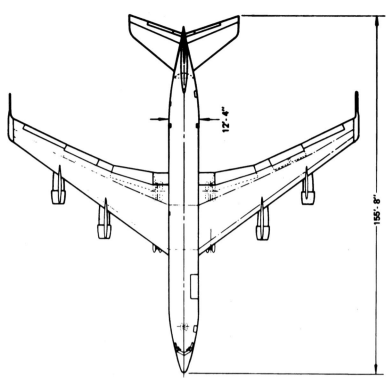
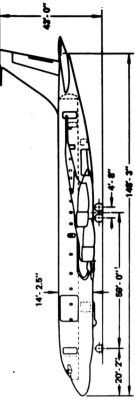
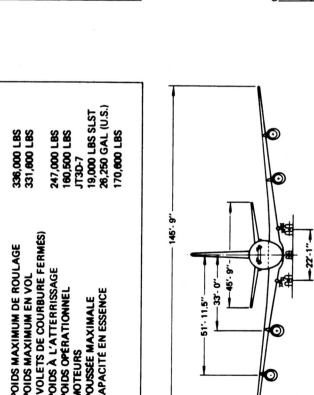

MAXIMUM TAXI WT	336,000 LB
MAXIMUM FLIGHT WEIGHT	331,600 LB
(FLAPS UP)	
DESIGN LANDING WT	247,000 LB
OPERATING WT	160,500 LB
ENGINES	JT3D-7
MAXIMUM THRUST RATING	19,000 LB SLST
FUEL CAPACITY	26,250 GAL (U.S.)
	170,600 LB

POIDS MAXIMUM DE ROULAGE	336,000 LBS
POIDS MAXIMUM EN VOL	331,600 LBS
(VOLETS DE COURBURE FERMÉS)	
POIDS À L'ATTERRISSAGE	247,000 LBS
POIDS OPÉRATIONNEL	160,500 LBS
MOTEURS	JT3D-7
POUSSÉE MAXIMALE	19,000 LBS SLST
CAPACITÉ EN ESSENCE	26,250 GAL (U.S.)
	170,600 LBS

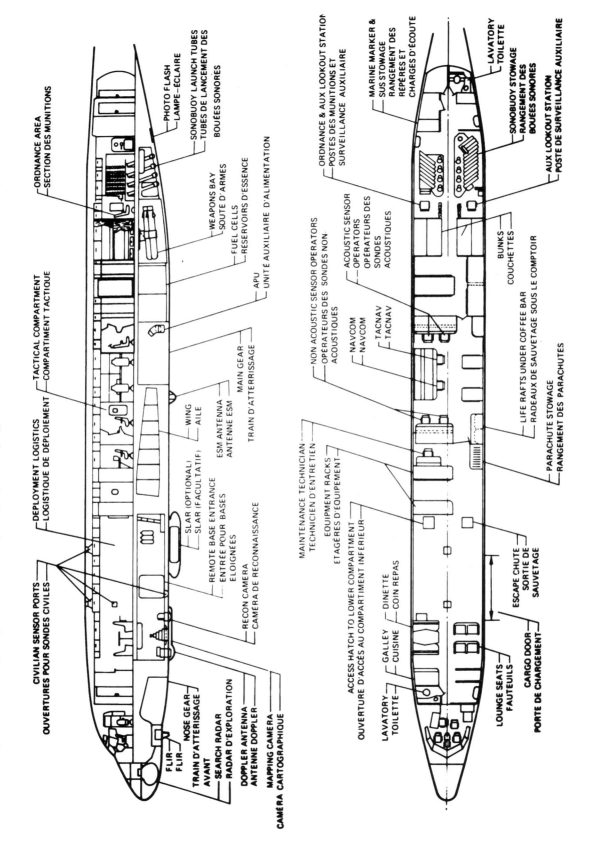

Interior arrangement of the Long Range Patrol Aircraft. (*Boeing Airplane Company*)

Boeing CC137 (707-347C)

conversion to long range troop transport, to supplement the five CC137 aircraft, was also a requirement. As a tanker, the LRPA would be able to transfer 20,000 lb. more fuel than the CC137.

A certain amount of offset benefits to the Canadian Aerospace Industry was also built into the equation. For the Long Range Maritime Patrol aircraft (LRMP), projected for the Australian requirement, those parts of the airframe and avionics package common to the LRPA would be built in Canada as well. The other factor in favour of the Boeing proposal was the commonality with the CC137 (707-347C) already in service with the Canadian Forces in the long range transport role.

In spite of these advantages, the lengthy runway requirements and marginal performance during sustained operation at low altitudes combined with the accelerated airframe fatigue from operating in that environment acted against the choice of the 707-LRPA. The contract, after many false starts and delays, was finally awarded to the Lockheed Aircraft Company for a variant of the P-3 Orion. A fleet of 18 of these aircraft eventually entered service with the Canadian Forces as the CP140 Aurora. An additional three "white tail" P-3C Orion aircraft were purchased later for crew training and northern patrol duties. These entered service as the CP140A Arcturus.

Canadian Forces CP140 Aurora aircraft 140101 in the original finish scheme and markings.
(DND Neg. No. GD81-0613)

CHAPTER NINE
Modelling the Boeing CC137 and NATO E-3 Sentry AWACS

Model of the Boeing CC137 in the definitive finish and marking scheme using the Heller 707-320B kit and Leading Edge Decals CC137 set with the wingtip refueling pods. (See also photograph on next page)

(Model by A. Stachiw)

Boeing CC137 (707-347C)

MODELS IN 1:72 SCALE

The Boeing 707 has been issued as the 707-320B by Heller. This is the same variant as the CC137, but without the cargo door on the forward port side of the fuselage. The modeller may also use the Airfix or Heller E-3 AWACS kit, since the E-3 is based on the 707-320B airframe.

Kits

Airfix Boeing E-3A /E-3D AWACS: The engines and pylons are included to represent both variants. The modeller can model the E-3A variant to represent the NATO AWACS without changes, or the CC137, by eliminating the radome. The basic aircraft used in the E-3 Sentry series is the Boeing 707-320B.

Heller Boeing 707-320B: This kit is representative of the CC137, lacking only the cargo door on the port side of the forward fuselage.

Heller Boeing E-3B/E-3D Sentry AWACS: The E-3B variant of this kit is representative of the E-3A Sentry in NATO service. One kit issue provided markings for the 50th Anniversary of NATO.

Model of the Boeing CC137 in the definitive finish and marking scheme using the Heller 707-320B kit and Leading Edge Decals CC137 set with the wingtip refueling pods.
(Model by A. Stachiw)

CHAPTER NINE

Model by Bill Scobie of the Boeing CC137, again in the definitive finish and marking scheme using the Heller 707-320B kit and Leading Edge Decals CC137 set with the wingtip refueling pods.
(Bill Scobie)

Pro Models Boeing CC137: This kit, a reboxed Heller Boeing 707-320B is representative of the CC137.

Aftermarket Products

Eduard Photoetch: AWACS aircraft details
Eduard Express-masks: Canopy and wheel masks.

Decals: JBOT Decals www.jbot.ca
JBOT has prepared a decal sheet depicting the CC137 aircraft in all marking schemes, including the "retirement" scheme, all with the window patterns.

A standard NATO AWACS sheet, and the NATO 50th Anniversary sheet are available as well.

Boeing CC137 (707-347C)

Leading Edge Decals: www.lemdecal.com
The original issue, which included the wing tip mounted refuelling pods, offered the interim markings, featuring the CANADA shadow lettering, as well as the definitive marking scheme with the CANADA WORDMARK, and window patterns.

MODELS IN 1:100 SCALE

The modeller can represent both the CC137 and the NATO E-3A Sentry AWACS with the Nitto/Entex kits. These kits are out of production.

Kits

Nitto/Entex 707-320C: This is a true representation of the CC137 in CF service.

Nitto/Entex E-3A Sentry AWACS: This is representative of the E-3A Sentry in NATO service.

Decals: JBOT Decals www.jbot.ca
JBOT has prepared a decal sheet depicting the CC137 aircraft in all marking schemes, including the "retirement" scheme, all with the window patterns.

A standard NATO AWACS sheet, and the NATO 50th Anniversary sheet are available as well.

MODELS IN 1:125 SCALE

Heller has released a 707-300B in 1:125 scale.

Kits

Heller 707-300B: Issued with Lufthansa markings. This kit is representative of the CC137, lacking only the cargo door on the port side of the forward fuselage. The door outline is featured on the available decal sets.

Decals: JBOT DECALS
http://members.rogers.com/jbot6/www.jbot.ca
JBOT has prepared a decal sheet depicting the CC137 aircraft in all marking schemes, including the "retirement" scheme, all with the window patterns.

A standard NATO AWACS sheet, and the NATO 50th Anniversary sheet are available as well.

MODELS IN 1:144 SCALE

In 1:144 scale, the Boeing 707 was released by Airfix as a CC137 with early Canadian Armed Forces markings. The kit was originally issued as a 707-420, the Rolls Royce Conway powered variant used by B.O.A.C. (British Overseas Airways Corporation). Academy has issued several boxings of the 707-300 variant, which as of 2002 were taken over by Minicraft. Revell issued a USAF E-3A Sentry AWACS in 1:144 scale, but the kit was based on a 707-120 model, which is totally inaccurate. However, the modeller could use the radome from this kit to convert the other kits to the AWACS configuration

Kits

Minicraft Boeing VC137C: An accurate representation of the CC137, lacking only the cargo door on the port side of the forward fuselage.

Airfix Boeing CC137: No longer available as a CC137, but still issued as a 707-420 series aircraft. Basically representative of the CC137 except for ventral strake (which is not on CC137), and the short vertical stabilizer. The modeller must modify the jet engine pods to represent the JT-3D pods, and modify the port outer engine pylon to the correct configuration. The kit decals represented the original bilingual marking scheme, but should be discarded in favour of the aftermarket JBOT decal sheet.

Revell Boeing E-3A AWACS: No longer available. The kit was inaccurate, being based on the smaller 707-120 variant, and was slightly out of scale. It featured USAF E-3A Sentry markings. The modeller could salvage the AWACS components and combine them with the Minicraft VC137C kit to more accurately depict the AWACS aircraft.

Decals: JBOT Decals www.jbot.ca
JBOT has prepared a decal sheet depicting the CC137 aircraft in all marking schemes, including the "retirement" scheme, all with the window patterns.

A standard NATO AWACS sheet, and the NATO 50th Anniversary sheet are available as well.

MODELS IN 1:200 / 1:400 SCALES

Decals: JBOT Decals www.jbot.ca
JBOT has prepared a decal sheet depicting the CC137 aircraft in all marking schemes, including the "retirement" scheme, all with the window patterns. These decals are designed for use on cast metal models, which are also produced in 1:400, and 1:500 scales.

BIBLIOGRAPHY

437 Squadron History: *The Military 707*. Seattle, WA: Boeing Commercial Airplane Co., 1985.

Boeing 707 Tanker/Transport. Wichita, KN: Boeing Military Airplane Company, nd.

"Boeing's 720 Testbed." *Aviation Week & Space Technology*. Sep.11, 1972. Supports ASW bid.

Boeing Transport Aircraft in Government and Defense Applications. Seattle, WA: Boeing Commercial Airplane Co., nd.

The Boeing Model 707-700. Seattle, WA: Boeing Commercial Airplane Co., nd.

CFM56: Maintenance. cfm international; SNECMA France & General Electric Co., USA. January, 1980.

CFM56: Executive Summary. cfm international; SNECMA France & General Electric Co., USA. March, 1983.

Lloyd, Alwyn T. "Boeing 707 & AWACS in Detail & Scale." *Aero*, 1987.

Stachiw, T. "In Canadian Service: Boeing 707." (Ottawa) *Airforce*, 1985.